THE HOUSEWIFE HANDYPERSON

BY JACQUELYN PEAKE

TAB BOOKS
Blue Ridge Summit, Pa. 17214

FIRST EDITION

FIRST PRINTING—DECEMBER 1977

Copyright 1977 by TAB BOOKS

Printed in the United States
of America

Library of Congress Cataloging in Publication Data

Peake, Jacqueline.
    The housewife handyperson.

    Includes index.
    1. Repairing—Amateurs' manuals. I. Title.
TT151.P4   643'.7   77-15974
ISBN 0-8306-7880-8
ISBN 0-8306-6880-2 pbk.

Contents

Cedar—Reviving a Refrigerator—Fixing Slippery Basement or Porch Steps—Painting Wicker Furniture—Painting Window Screens—Painting Over Surfaces in Poor or Unprepared Condition—Painting Masonry—Painting Exterior Trim, Windows, Doors, Porches and Steps—Painting Particlebaord—Painting Hardboard—Simulating Stucco With Paint—Bleaching Light-Colored Woodwork—Staining—Mini-Items to Save Time and Temper When Painting

Introduction

As a child, there was always Daddy or the boy next door to repair our skates or bicycle, and somehow many of us women have gotten into the habit of thinking it takes a male mind to fathom anything that involves mechanics or construction. T'aint so, girls! You can manage your home and automobile very nicely yourself, with a little help, and still retain your famininity. Most men really admire a woman who can handle an emergency without panicking, or can fix little things that go wrong around the house. It behooves your sanity and your bank account to be able to take care of these minor repairs. And take it from a gal who's been there—*you can do it!*

This book can save women—single or married women—hundreds of dollars in repair bills every year, plus many, many precious hours. Keep this little volume handy. It'll show you how to take care of a thousand and one minor disasters that are always happening around every house or apartment. It won't tell you how to re-roof the house or give the old Edsel a ring job. These tasks belong to the experts. But, it will show you how to make a door stop dragging a trench across the living room carpet; what to do and not to do when the Edsel boils over; and how to spruce up that miserable kitchen linoleum, plus hundreds of other useful bits of knowledge.

Wasting money on needless repair bills is not efficient or smart. Why pay a plumber (whose take-home pay is probably triple yours) for a simple little job like putting in a new faucet washer? With these instructions, you can do it yourself in less than an hour. And think how happy your husband would be to come home from a long hard day's work to find that *you* had fixed the dripping faucet!

I once had a dear teacher, a Mrs. Vincent, who taught me many little truths and bits of practical knowledge as she guided me through grammar school. Those were depression days and we lived in what would now be considered a poverty-stricken area. Mrs. Vincent had little equipment and less cash to run her tiny rural school, but she more than made up for the lack with her boundless energy, wit, and determination. She taught us by proverbs and maxims, liberally laced with practical examples. The one I remember best was, "Necessity is the mother of invention." (I can still make a very attractive and serviceable rug from *corn husks*. We learned this homely craft because some of the children came from homes where bare, packed earth was the only floor their homes could boast.) Through the years, this maxim has come back again and again, chiding me to be inventive and flexible.

Some of the repairs and ideas I describe in this book will be far from orthodox, but so what? You're not applying for admission to the carpenter's local. You just want to get those traverse rods hung, and if my way is a little different from the way everybody else does it, it's because I've discovered a method that seems simpler and easier to manage.

This little book will teach you many things about tools, carpentry, plumbing, your automobile, general maintenance of your home, and a host of miscellany that I couldn't seem to fit into any of the regular chapters. Add what's here to the magic ingredient of your own ingenuity and nothing can stop you!

Read on, and good luck!

Jacquelyn Peake

Equipment

**Hammers, Hardware Store Owners,
and Other Useful Tools You Should Know About**

In order to take care of your home you will need this book, a
few basic tools, and all the help you can get. The book you
have. Tools will be covered in this chapter. Now, a word to the
wise about the help. *Get to know your neighborhood hardware
dealer.* Bat your eyes and look sweetly helpless, if you're so
inclined. Smile and wave whenever you pass his shop, if that's
more your style. Bake him a cake for National Hardware
Week. Just be sure he knows and likes you. This unassuming
gentleman is a vast storehouse of knowledge and can be your
best friend when it comes to expert advice on repairs. He
knows what you can safely attempt and what you should leave
to the professionals. He'll sell you the right tool or part for the
job, and give you free instructions on how to use it. He is
absolutely invaluable.

The basic tools you'll probably need in order to handle
most home repairs include a hammer and nails, a nail set,
screwdrivers and screws, an awl, pliers, a plunger and toilet
auger, adhesives, household oil, household paraffin, a
yardstick, a saw, and a drill. Don't let this formidable list send
you running to apply for a room at the YWCA, and, on the other
hand, don't rush out and buy everything at once. Buy the tools
as you need them. As you become more proficient (and

confident!) about fixing things up around the house, you may even want to add a few more sophisticated tools.

A word to the wise. Don't cheat yourself by buying cheap tools. A 98¢ hammer is no bargain if the handle splinters the first time you give it a good lick. But, it certainly isn't necessary to buy that impressive (and heavy!) $9.95 one either. That's for the professional carpenter. Somewhere in the middle price range is usually a good buy for the amateur repairwoman. The one I use cost $2.96 and has performed beautifully for years, helping me put up shelves in the basement, make deck furniture from scrap lumber, and even install some badly needed gutters on the eaves.

THE HAMMER

That hammer should be the first tool you buy. You'll find two types on the shelves. One has straight claws, the other's claws are slightly curved. You want the latter. You'll also notice two different types of *faces* (the business end). One is slightly convex and is called a *bell face*. The other is *flat*. The bell face is a little more difficult to work with because you need more skill in hitting the nail straight with it. But, if you should miss and strike the surface of your work, it doesn't do too much damage so I think it's perferable. The flat face is simple to use, but, if you miss with it, you're going to make a great big ugly dent in your work. Get a medium weight hammer, about 12 or 14 ounces.

Although you'll discover many other uses as time goes on, the obvious purposes of a hammer are to drive and pull nails. To drive a nail, hold it upright in your left hand (if you're right-handed), pointed end pressed firmly against the wood. Grasp the hammer about midway down the handle and tap the nail lightly several times. This will force it down into the wood far enough for you to let go. You're liable to bang your fingers if you hold on too long. Now, keeping your eye on the nail, not the hammer, strike again, more vigorously this time. If the nail tends to lean, tap it lightly on the side to straighten, then continue striking until it is nearly flush with the surface of your work. If you're merely nailing a porch step down, finish off with a couple of really hard whacks. If the work must have a nice, smooth appearance, you'll need to use a nail set. (More on this a few paragraphs down.)

To pull a nail without marring the wood, place a piece of scrap wood or a thick wad of cloth against the surface of the work and next to the nail. Push the nail's shank into the curved claws of your hammer, rest the hammer's head on the scrap of wood or pad of cloth, and pull toward you.

NAILS

Nails come in different sizes and are gauged according to a graduated system based on *pennyweight*. A ten-penny nail is larger than a six-penny nail which is larger than a two-penny nail. But, you don't need to strain your brain trying to learn the relative sizes. Just go in and ask the lumber or hardware dealer to let you see his selection. Then, ask for "a pound of those," pointing to the size that looks right to you for the job. If you're not sure of which size you need, tell him what your current project is and he'll suggest the correct nail.

Nails also come in different types. *Finish* nails are for finish work and they have very small heads. *Common* nails are for rough work or work that must be very sturdy and have large, flat heads (easy to hit, incidentally). There are also *concrete* nails for nailing things to concrete, but it takes a powerful arm muscle to drive one in. I can't do it.

THE NAIL SET

A nail set is a small tool about the size and shape of those pencils that hang on key chains. It has a broad flat end, a shank, and a pointed end. It is used to avoid hammer marks on wood. When your nail has been driven to within one-quarter inch or so of the wood, place the nail set, pointed end in contact with the nail head, and carefully strike the opposite flat end with the hammer (Fig. 1-1). In a few strokes the nail head will

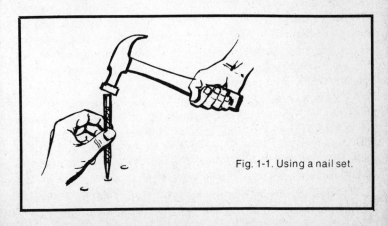

Fig. 1-1. Using a nail set.

be pushed below the surface and you won't have marred the finish with hammer marks. The slight hole which results above the nail head is usually filled with wood putty and sanded to blend with the rest of the wood.

SCREWDRIVERS

Screwdrivers are exceptionally useful tools. Although many men scream in anguish at the heretical thought, I find screwdrivers invaluable for prying things apart, acting as levers to lift things, and driving holes in Sheetrock for inserting Molly Screws (more about those in the chapter on walls). Really, I think it's cheaper in the long run to replace a screwdriver that has finally become blunted through multiple (and unorthodox) uses than to buy a whole array of tools that are only used once in a blue moon.

The screwdriver you're probably most familiar with is the slot type. It has a blunt, squared off end and is used on screws with one slot. Because there are many sizes of screws you'll encounter, I'd suggest buying two screwdrivers (they're not expensive), one small and one large. You'll also need a Phillips screwdriver. This kind has a pointed tip that flares back into four cross-shaped ridges. Almost all electrical appliances and many pieces of furniture are put together with Phillips screws, identified by a little criss-cross hole instead of a slot. Just buy one medium-sized Phillips screwdriver since you can most likely use it for any Phillips screw you run across.

As you progress from simple repairs to more complicated projects you may want to add a spiral-ratchet ("Yankee") screwdriver to your tool box. This is a great wrist saver when you have many screws to insert. A Yankee screwdriver has a bulbous wooden handle, and a spiraled shaft. It drives the screw in by a plunger action. In fact, it works very much like those spinning toys that children make whirl around the floor and hum by pushing a handle up and down.

PLIERS

You'll want a pair of slip-joint pliers, too. Slip-joint pliers have a slot at the pivot point that allows the pliers to be adjusted for wide or narrow widths. Move the handles one way along the slot and they'll grip wide objects but won't close all the way. Move them the other direction in the slot and they'll close all the way over small objects. Be sure you get a pair with a wire cutting edge, too. This is very handy. A pair of shearing edges inside the jaw can cut just about any wire you'll be dealing with.

Here again is a chance for any men who've wandered into the audience to stand up and scream: a good pair of pliers will often do the job which some purists declare demands an expensive wrench. So you do grind the nice sharp edges off a nut occasionally? Nuts are cheap. And, you can ususally avoid even this minor boo-boo by placing your thin rubber jar opener or a rag between the pliers' jaws and the nut.

PLUNGER AND TOILET AUGER

A plunger and toilet auger (or *snake*) can save you if the plumbing suddenly decides to clog up just minutes before the light of your life or your husband's boss is due to arrive for dinner. You'll need a four-inch plunger to use on the kitchen sink or bathroom lavatory if they get sluggish or completely stopped up. The toilet auger is, obviously, for the toilet.

The plunger is a cup-shaped rubber device attached to a wooden handle. You've probably heard it called *a plumber's friend*. The plunger is placed over the clogged drain and worked up and down vigorously in order to create suction in the drain and clear out the obstruction. The auger is a strange-looking contraption consisting of a wooden handle, a bent shank, and about five feet of coiled wire that can reach down into the toilet trap. You put the auger into the toilet bowl and begin turning the handle. The twisting action of the wire going round and round can dislodge almost anything. There'll be a more complete discussion of these two tools and how to use them in the chapter on plumbing.

ADHESIVES, OIL, AND OTHER HELPS

Although not technically tools, you should also have on hand a bottle of white glue, a can of household oil, tubes (it takes a combination of two) of epoxy glue, a block of household paraffin, and a yardstick (free from most lumberyards). Liquid steel is great, too, when you have to join or repair metal. It comes in a tube and hardens into real metal on contact with the air. It'll seal small holes, join broken pieces and can even be used in craftwork since it's easily moldable before it dries.

SAWS

A small handsaw is nice to have on hand for *very* small cutting jobs such as trimming a closet rod to size, and only if you don't anticipate doing very much else. Hand sawing, to my way of thinking, is just plain exhausting, and it makes much more sense to invest in an electric saber saw. This is a real fun tool and almost every man's workshop has one because it's so versatile. You should have one, too, because it's lightweight, exceptionally safe, and can cut everything from a solid oak door to a frozen rump roast. With a little practice you can even cut fancy curves with it.

Instead of having a frightening, whirling blade, the saber saw has a slender cutting edge which moves up and down, thousands of times a minute, in a vibrating motion. It glides along the work on a flat base with the blade extending down several inches below the saw itself. There are no cutting surfaces above the work where your precious hands are—a most important safety feature.

Your saber saw will come with a selection of blades in various sizes. Those with the coarsest teeth are for cutting *soft* materials; those with finer teeth are for cutting *hard* materials, such as soft metals. The blade cuts on the up stroke, so put the good side of your material down for the best looking cut. Some woods, particularly plywood, have a tendency to splinter when cut. You can avoid this by putting a piece of transparent tape over the cutting line, or coating the line with shellac.

DRILLS

A hand drill is fine for drilling small holes in wood or metal. It looks something like a rotary eggbeater. There's a wooden handle for your left hand, a crank for your right hand, and gears that turn a drill bit. The bit fits into a chuck (a gripping device) that can be adjusted to accommodate bits of different sizes. To use it, you make a small pilot hole with your awl (a simple tool resembling a stubby ice pick), place the drill bit in the hole, and slowly begin turning the crank. As soon as you've made a respectable size hole you can speed up the action.

If your finances allow it, though, get an electric drill. It's a great companion for your saber saw and a real work saver. This little powerhouse can be adapted to almost any woodworking operation you can dream up (sanding, buffing, polishing, paint mixing) by adding attachments. But, naturally, you'll use it most often for drilling. Mine has come into use dozens of times, too, for things that the average carpenter would never think of—like drilling a hole in the end of my broom so it'll hang on a nail in the broom closet, making shallow holes in the trunk of my Christmas tree one year so the little screws in the tree-holder would go in better and, the same Christmas, drilling little holes in the flat end of pine cones to speed up the making of a wreath for the front door. (Put a squirt of white glue in the holes, stick a large cocktail-size toothpick in the hole and let dry. Next day stick these into a Styrofoam wreath, finish off with some artificial flocked fruit, and you'll have the best looking wreath on the block. There—that's my Christmas present to you for *this* year!)

All electric drills come with a set of vari-sized bits. These are the little spiraled tools that do the work. You just select the one that's right for your need, fit it into the chuck, and drill away.

Just a word of caution, though. Both the saber saw and electric drill work so rapidly that you can easily cut past your mark or gouge out an irreparable hole before you know it. Practice, practice, practice on scrap material before you begin refinishing that heirloom chest you picked up at the Salvation Army thrift shop.

Either of these tools will cost from $20 to $30, depending upon what the traffic will bear in your area. But, if you watch the hardware sales, you can often pick them up for half that.

And, of course, there're always birthdays, Christmas, anniversaries, anniversary-of-the-day-we-met, etc. Don't be shy about asking outright for a drill set. Your father, husband, son, or boyfriend may think you've finally gone around the bend, but if you explain sweetly that you'll be very careful and will undoubtedly save many of your hard-earned dollars, your benefactor will probably see the light. I have a friend who acquired a set as a divorce present from her ex-husband—unusual, but practical, all things considered.

This ploy can be worked for other do-it-yourselfer goodies, too. I heard about another ambitious young lady who told her mother all she wanted for her birthday was 14 bags of Sakrete to finish the patio with! She got them, too.

As I've said, with a little natural ingenuity you can do anything!

2

Doors & Windows

**How to Keep Them Working
So the Cold Stays Out and the
Deliveryman From Tiffany's Can Get In!**

No matter where you live, whether it's in a dream apartment in New York or a 1920 bungalow in Omaha, you have doors and windows. And the chances are better than even that these doors and windows occasionally stick, rattle, sag, break, leak, or need some drapery. Here are a few hints to make living with them a bit easier.

WINDOWS THAT JAM

Violins and good wine become better with age; most windows just get cranky—especially if they've been mistreated or neglected over the years. If you find your double-hung windows sticking, jamming, and generally making life difficult whenever you need a breath of air, try rubbing the track with a block of household paraffin. Then, take a rag and rub the paraffin briskly until it coats the wood and some is absorbed into the wood fibers. This will form a thin, smooth film for the window to ride on. Things should go better for both of you after this treatment.

WINDOWS STUCK TIGHT WITH PAINT

Occasionally, some dum-dum will decide to paint a window but will be too lazy to do the job right. The result, which you may inherit, is a window which absolutely refuses to open because it's stuck shut with paint. After reading the chapter in this book on painting, *you* would never do such a thing, but that doesn't solve the problem of the window enameled shut by your predecessor.

You can nearly always open these stubborn windows with a little effort. First, take a sharp knife and run it all around the edges, cutting through as much of the paint as possible. This probably won't free the window, but you should give it a good shove, anyway, to see. Then, go outside and stick your biggest screwdriver or a chisel underneath the sash. Use your hammer to drive it in just a bit. Take hold of the tool's handle and give it a good heave downward, using the blade as a lever to pry the window up. Try several times along the bottom edge of the window.

If this doesn't free it, go back inside and hammer the screwdriver into the track between the sash and the stop. Carefully rock the screwdriver back and forth. This is possible because there's always a little space here. Do this in several places. Again, try to lift the window.

As a last resort, if the thing is still stuck, get a thick block of wood or a brick padded with rags and hold it against the sash. Carefully tap the block with your hammer, moving the block along and tapping until you've gone all the way around. If one time around doesn't do it, go around again, tapping a little harder. (Just be careful not to let that hammer slip so that you break a pane!) You're almost guaranteed results with this last-ditch method. And, if you *should* break a pane...instructions for relief follow in a few pages.

SLIDING DOORS THAT JAM

The paraffin trick for unsticking also helps to make balky sliding or folding doors easier to live with. Sometimes, though, a sliding door will bind so badly along the lower edge that it's almost impossible to operate. This is often because the door has dropped down from its upper guides. In closet doors, you get inside and locate some metal plates on the top of the doors. They'll have a slot and nut in them and should be just below the rollers. Loosen the nut with your pliers, lift the door a bit, and stick a few magazines under it to hold it in place. Then, tighten the nut again, a half-inch or so *farther down in the slot* than it was before. This should raise the door enough to let it slide easily.

SLIDING SCREEN DOORS THAT JAM

Some sliding doors, particularly screen doors that go with plate glass patio doors, have their adjustment on the bottom rollers. These doors are absolutely abominable because when gravity and the weight of the door move the adjustment nut down, the top rollers naturally drop out of the track and there's nowhere for the door to go but out. I had a screen door once that spent a whole summer doing this, jumping the track at least once a day and landing horizontally across what I laughingly called my garden. I was very young then and knew little of the ways of fixing things, so I had to depend on a pleasant old gentleman next door to put it back for me each time. Finally, as the leaves were turning gold and the pumpkins filling out for their annual orgy, the man explained to me, in desperation and in words of one syllable, the facts of life concerning sliding screen doors.

You take the screen out of the frame by lifting it up and out of the bottom track. Lay it flat on the ground with the adjustment nut on the upper side facing you. Loosen the nut and *lower* the roller a bit, tighten the screw, and slide the door back into the frame, top side first, then bottom side.

It was amazingly easy once I knew how. Of course, by then it was winter and I wasn't using the screens anyway. But the knowledge came in handy the next summer.

WOBBLY SCREEN DOORS

Screen doors, with age, often become wobbly and completely *out of square*, to use a good old carpenter's term. They drag across the floor, have gaps around the frame large enough for an army of mosquitoes and flies to sail through, and are a general pain the the neck. If you have such a gem, and it isn't too far gone, you can repair it with inexpensive corner braces. These are little flat pieces of metal about 3/4 inch wide, with two arms at right angles that extend three or four inches. They have pre-drilled holes in them. They usually come packaged in sets of two or four and are found in the hardware department of your dime store, or at the hardware store, naturally. You'll need four braces, one for each corner of the door.

Take the door down off the framework. It's probably held up by two hinges which are screwed both to the door and the framework. Unscrew the side of the hinge that's on the framework. Lay the door on a flat surface and "square up" the corners. If you can find a carpenter's square to use, borrow it. This tool is great for getting corners exactly square. But, lacking one, improvise a substitute. I fixed a screen door once using a newspaper as a square. All you need is something to lay under the door to help get the corners square. Just line up the edges of the door with the edges of the newspaper and you're in business.

The joints in the wood will probably have pulled apart a bit, so squirt a generous shot of glue into each joint before you proceed. This will help to keep it square once it's fixed.

Put a brace in one corner about two inches in from the edge, tap the joints together with your hammer and get the corner square. Then, screw the brace to the door with medium-sized screws. This is usually pretty easy because screen doors aren't made of very hard wood. Repeat for the other three corners. Rehang the door on the framework and you should have a much better behaved door!

SLIDING DOORS THAT JUMP THE TRACK

When a sliding door jumps the track, it is often because something got in the way as you closed it, forcing a rear roller up and out of the track. Most of these units have some little guides screwed to the floor, one in the center and one on each side of each door. Unscrew the ones on the room side of the door and take them off. Lift the offending door and get it back on the track by holding the door up and at an angle, slipping the rollers back onto the track. As you let the door down to a vertical position, the rollers will catch in the track and you're back in business. Replace the guides and clean out all that junk on the floor of the closet so it won't happen again!

DOORS THAT DRAG ON THE FLOOR

If a door just binds a bit at the bottom, you can usually stop it by laying a sheet of medium grade sandpaper rough side up on the floor or sill (wherever the door is dragging) and opening and closing the door across the sandpaper a few times. This will usually take off enough wood to make the door operate smoothly.

However, sometimes a door will drag across the floor, scraping an arc of bare wood or making a regular trench in the carpet. The first thing to do is check the hinges. They do wear loose with time and it's amazing what a difference tightening them can sometimes make. With your screwdriver try to turn each screw (clockwise) in the hinge a little tighter. Then check the door for fit. If the screws slip around as you turn them and never get tight, it's because the holes have worn too big. This problem is remedied by removing the screw completely, sticking a couple of wooden toothpicks into the hole, giving it a squirt of glue, and replacing the screw. It ought to behave then. You're probably wondering why I don't just suggest using a larger screw. This would seem logical, I know, except that the holes in the hinges probably won't take a bigger one.

If the door is still dragging after all that, you're going to have to take a little off the bottom edge. This involves taking the door off the framework.

To take the door down, you must separate the hinges into two parts. Almost all hinges have big metal pins holding them together. These pins have a knob-like top and are inserted from the top of the hinge. When you remove this pin, the hinge will separate and the door will come away from the frame. Get a friend to help you with this job. It's pretty hard to hammer away at a contrary hinge pin (and, believe me, most of them are contrary) and hold up a heavy door at the same time.

Take your screwdriver and place its tip just underneath the head of the pin. Then, hammer away from below. If you're lucky, this will loosen it enough that it can be lifted out. If not, then it's probably stuck from many layers of old paint. Go get your fingernail polish remover and pour a spoonful or two down the hinge. Be sure to protect the floor with newspapers or old rags. Open and close the door a few times to work the polish remover down into the hinge. Let it set a few minutes, then pour a little more in around the top of the pin (which is where it will be *really* stuck). This ought to soften the paint enough to let you hammer the pin out.

Remove the hinge pins and lift the door down. Decide how much has to come off the bottom—it probably won't be more than a half-inch. Make a mark across the bottom at that measurement using your awl and yardstick. This is your cutting guide.

Place the door across two sawhorses if you have them, or some chairs, the patio table, or whatever you can find that will give you a sturdy base to work on. Have the bottom edge of the door to your right, put your left knee and left hand on the door to brace it, and cut away from you with your saber saw, following that cutting guide. If you don't have an electric saw, take the door to a lumberyard and ask someone there to cut it for you. The fee will be small.

Seal the raw cut with shellac or paint to retard moisture absorption and replace the door on its hinges.

DOORS THAT DON'T FIT THE FRAME

Extreme dampness is usually the reason a door suddenly becomes too big for its frame and won't close properly. You can just about bank on this being the case if it happens on the day the bottom dropped out at 3:00 p.m. and you needed an oar instead of a bus token to get home from work. In this case, all you should do is sand down the latch edge with sandpaper *very* slightly. If a few minutes of this treatment doesn't make it fit, then forget it and wait for dry weather. If you take off too much, there'll be a big gaping hole there when it shrinks back to normal.

If the door won't close in dry weather, it's a different ball of wax, and the first thing you should check for are loose hinges. (There's an explanation of this procedure a few paragraphs back.) If the hinges are tight and the door still strikes the frame, then you need to do a little minor surgery. You're going to take that door off its hinges and set them deeper into the woodwork. Don't panic, students. This is really no more challenging than explaining to a policeman just why you felt it necessary to make that left turn on red.

First, look around the house until you find something sturdy to slip under the open door while you operate. Try a paperback book (not this one, you need the directions!), a pie pan or a few back issues of *Cosmopolitan*. The idea is to keep the door from sagging when you get it off that first hinge.

Slip the book or what-have-you under the door and jam it in firmly. With your screwdriver, remove the screws from the part of the lower hinge that is attached to the *door frame*. Don't touch the part of the hinge that is attached to the door itself. Fold the half of the hinge you just unscrewed out of the way.

Look squarely at the little rectangle that has been gouged out of the wood in the frame by some previous carpenter. This is called a *mortise*—just a fancy name for a place to set the hinge. You are simply going to make the door sit one-quarter inch or so farther away from the place it's striking. In the process, the door should stop striking! Nothing hard about that, is there?

Buy or borrow a chisel. (In a pinch you *could* use your extra large screwdriver but it takes longer that way.)Standing in the doorway, facing the frame, place the chisel's edge at one edge of the mortise and hit the chisel's handle a sharp blow with your hammer. This will make a sharp cut into the wood. Move the chisel over a bit and do the same thing until you've made a cut about one-quarter inch deep all around the outline of the mortise. Now, with your chisel and hammer, this time held as closely as possible to a position *parallel* to the mortise, gouge out a slice of wood about one-quarter inch thick from the mortise.

Put the hinge back in place, reset the screws and tighten them. Then, repeat the whole process for the top hinge. When you're through, the door will sit firmly one-quarter inch farther away from the latch frame, and should fit.

If your door just strikes the frame at the lower or upper edge and seems to fit otherwise, just reset the hinge at the end that's striking. Now, sit down, and admire your cleverness.

Sometimes your problem is just the opposite of the above: the door has shrunk until there's a sizable gap between the edge of the door and the frame. Many times this is the reason a latch won't hold properly.

What you do in this case is a process called *shimming*. Instead of making the mortises deeper, you're going to build them up. It's exactly the same procedure as above, from the paperback book through removing the screws of the lower hinge. But, instead of cutting the mortise *deeper* you're going to make the original cut *shallower*.

Locate some filler material. Heavy cardboard will do for interior doors, very thin wood for exterior doors. Cut several pieces the same size and shape as the face of the mortise, from the filler material. Put them into the mortise using the size of the gap to determine how many you need, replace the hinge, and reset the screws. This will reduce the gap considerably.

WARPED DOORS

Dampness, again, is usually the culprit when a door warps. You'll know it's warped when the door strikes the frame on the *hinge* edge. It probably won't close all the way, either, because of a bow in the middle of the door. And a door doesn't have to be old to warp, either—some of the lightweight hollow-core doors (just a square framework with a thin piece of plywood nailed to each side) used today in modestly priced homes are a natural for this problem. I had to repair one not long ago and it was in a house less than a year old. The door warped because it was the one to my laundry room where steam from the washer and dryer created a tremendous amount of dampness.

To get a warped door back into line isn't hard, but it helps to have a strong friend around. You'll need to buy a hinge to install in the *middle* of the door's edge, between the two hinges that are already there. For appearance's sake, try to match the ones already there as closely as possible.

Now, if you want to do a really professional-looking job, you can cut mortises for the hinge (as described in the directions above), but it isn't absolutely necessary. The door will work just as well if you set the hinges on the surface of the wood—and it's certainly less work.

Measure the distance between the two existing hinges until you find the exact middle. This is where you'll put the new hinge. Place one side of the hinge against the edge of the door at that point and, with a pencil, put a mark in each screw hole. Drill a small pilot hole on each of these pencil marks, put the hinge back up and screw it into place.

Now, your strong friend comes into play. Have him or her push on the door until it is straight. Quickly, put the other half of the hinge on the frame where it is to go and make pencil marks through *those* screw holes. Your friend can relax now for a few minutes while you make the pilot holes for those screws. Again, have him or her push the door into place. This time you're going to screw the hinge to the door frame. Be sure to use sturdy screws that are plenty long because there'll be a good bit of pressure on this door until, with luck, it un-warps itself back into line.

DOORS AND WINDOWS THAT LEAK AIR

If your doors and windows rattle when the wind blows or if you can actually *feel* the wind coming in, then it's a sure sign you need to weatherstrip. This is the reason your home may be cold in winter even with the heat turned up to the top of the thermostat, or hot in summer with the air conditioner chugging away for all it's worth.

A heating contractor told me not long ago that the cracks around doors and windows in a unweatherstripped home can easily add up to a hole as big as a full-sized window open all the time. And he said that closing those gaps will save most people up to a hundred dollars a year in fuel bills alone, aside from the difference in comfort the people will feel. So, you can see that a few dollars spent on weatherstripping is a very good investment.

Your friend the hardware store owner stocks several types of weatherstripping intended for different jobs and differing degrees of efficiency. What you buy will depend upon your finances, how long you intend to stay in your home, and how much of a problem you have (whether there are really sizable gaps or just a hint of leakage).

The best, most expensive, and most permanent type of weatherstripping is a spring metal affair that comes in pre-cut strips. It has a flat edge about one-half inch wide that you nail to the door jamb. This flat part flares out into a springy section that presses against the door when it's shut, keeping out the wind. It's important to install spring metal weatherstripping with the springy edge just clearing the stop. (The stop is that long thin piece of wood nailed down the length of the door frame. It *stops* the door from going too far.) If the weatherstripping drags on the stop, it can't spring out against the door when it's shut.

This type of weatherstripping can also be installed on double-hung windows. Raise the bottom sash all the way and nail the stripping in the track where the sash slides. For appearance's sake, the little flat part should be closest to the room with the springy part toward the outside. Lower the sash and do the same for the top half. Just be sure the weatherstripping is long enough. If you cut it too short and there's an inch or so of space between the edge of the sash and the beginning of the weatherstripping, your window could easily get hung up when you try to raise or lower it.

The only real problem with spring metal weatherstripping comes if your doors and windows don't fit the pre-cut sizes. The metal is pretty hard to cut at home without proper equipment. So, take the exact measurements of your doors and windows with you to the store. If you decide on spring weatherstripping and the pre-cut sizes don't exactly jibe with your measurements, talk the man behind the counter into cutting it for you. He'll do it if you smile sweetly and explain how you're just freezing to death over there at your place and just don't think you can make it through another night with all that rain and snow blowing in on your bed.

Other types of weatherstripping are a little easier to manage, if not quite so permanent. You can get a plastic foam tape with adhesive back that is quite serviceable. You just peel off the paper backing and press it against the door stop. The pressure of the door against that foam-upholstered stop seals out the draft. This kind of weatherstripping is good for awning and casement windows, too, but not for double-hung windows. On awning and casement windows you press the adhesive back on the framework where the edge of the sash strikes.

Probably the least expensive weatherstripping for door and windows is felt. It comes in rolls and you tack it into place. But I don't recommend it unless you're only planning to stay at your place for a winter or two. It frays and has to be replaced very soon.

Although it is not technically weatherstripping, there is another keep-the-weather-out material you may need someday. It is a spongy soft rubber and comes in ropes of about one and one-half inch diameter. It's used to fill in spaces around such things as window air conditioners. You just cut off the amount you need and push it into the cracks.

Sometimes, with age, doors and windows will pull slightly away from the framework of the house itself, leaving space for wind, sand, and cold to blow into the house. *Caulking*, which is similar to weatherstripping in effect, is the answer to this problem.

Caulking, which is always installed from the outside, comes in several forms. The easiest type to use is called rope caulking. Logically, it comes in a rope form which you just press into the cracks with your fingers. It would probably be perfectly adequate for any repair you'd have to make. But you should know about the other types. Gun-grade caulking comes in cylinders about the size of a can of hair spray and is shot into the cracks through a nozzle. It is a semi-solid, sticky substance that makes a very secure seal. Most builders use gun-grade caulking. Knife-grade caulking is worked into the cracks with a putty knife, and I think it is the hardest to use, besides being the messiest.

DAMAGED WINDOW AND PORCH SCREENS

Screens are intended to keep the insect population where it belongs—outside—and these screens are as desirable as indoor plumbing in most parts of this country. Many homes have screened-in porches or window screens that are in a deplorable state of repair, though. For some reason, this is the last thing that gets fixed in many homes. Yet, mosquitoes have an absolute genius for locating the one tiny hole you hope no one will notice. Repairing torn or rusted screens is a job any woman can handle with ease, though.

When you're dealing with a very large expanse of screening, such as a portion of a porch, and there are only a couple of little holes, the sensible thing to do is repair instead of replace. There are two acceptable methods. For either one you have to buy some new screen wire at the hardware store. Sometimes you can get little packages of patch-size pieces, but only the very largest dealers carry these. You'll probably have to buy a piece off a large roll. You're only going to need a little, but they sell it by the foot and as wide as most windows, so you'll end up with plenty left over for the next job.

Method number one is to cut a square of screening about three times as big as the hole or tear. Fringe it all around by pulling out some of the wires, then bend the fringed ends over with your pliers until they are at right angles to the rest of the patch. Place this patch over the hole and push the bent ends through to the outside. Then, go out there and bend them down flat.

The second method is not according to Hoyle, perhaps, but a heck of a lot easier and just as permanent. Cut the patch as above, but don't fringe it. Lather its edges well with epoxy glue and simply press it into place. You may need to hold it in place until it dries. Try using a couple of hairpins stuck through the wire in some place where there's no glue.

You might also try mending very *tiny* holes— those not large enough to warrant a patch—with a bit of clear fingernail polish. Dab on a drop, let it dry, then dab on another.

For a window screen in really bad condition, you might just as well do a good job and replace the whole thing. Take the screen frame down and lay it on a flat surface. *Very carefully* pry off the moldings that are holding the old screen on. These are thin and break easily. With luck, they'll come off in one piece with the nails intact. Leave the nails in.

Measure the inside width and length of the area to be covered. Ask your dealer for a piece that size. If you're lucky, he may have a width which is just right. If not, you'll have to buy a larger width and cut it down. Try to get him to do it for you because you need heavy shears to do the job at home.

Place the screen wire on the frame and, stretching as you go, tack it down with carpet tacks. A staple gun is nice if you have one, but not essential. Then put the old molding back in place and nail it down.

Some screens need painting periodically. There's an easy way to do this and you'll find the directions in the chapter on painting.

BROKEN WINDOW PANES

Replacing a broken pane of glass isn't really as hard as it looks. First you measure the pane size *exactly* using a good metal tape or ruler...*not* a piece of string! Women have been tarred and feathered and run out of town by more than one glass cutter for showing up with a stretchy piece of butcher's twine and saying, "I want a piece of glass this wide." In order to get an exact measurement, you'll need to chip away all the old putty and broken glass. Putty, incidentally, is that dried clay-like substance all around the edges of the glass. After the window is clean, measure from top to bottom, side to side of the opening, and write the measurements down. *Don't* figure on just a bit extra "for good measure," because there's no way you can fit an 8 1/2″ × 10 1/2″ pane into an opening that's 8″ × 10″. 8″ × 10″.

Take these measurements with you to the glass company, and if you're lucky and have been living right, it will be a standard size and they'll have it in stock. Otherwise, you'll have to wait a few minutes while they cut one. Ask for a few *glazier's points* before you leave. These are tiny metal triangles used to hold the glass in place. You'll also need a small can of window putty. Get this at the hardware store or the dime store.

Home again, open that can of putty and put a layer of it all around the frame. This helps to seal the glass in place. Set the pane into the opening and secure it with the glazier's points. You take one and, holding it right next to the glass, push it down into the wood frame. Use a screwdriver or pencil eraser. The points are quite sharp and will go in easily (Fig. 2-1). Put at least two on each side of the pane.

Scoop out a few spoonsful of putty now and roll it around in the palm of your hand until you have a smooth ball. Then, put it on a table and roll it back and forth until you have a nice long "snake" (shades of kindergarten!). The "snake" is then

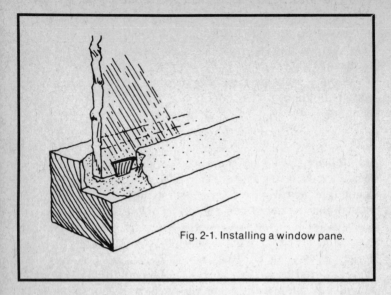
Fig. 2-1. Installing a window pane.

pressed all around the edges of the glass to form a firm, neat seal. Professional glass installers do it another way but I think this is simpler. Smooth the putty with your fingers (copying the other panes in the window), then clean off any that got up onto the glass. All done—and you've saved enough to see the best movie in town every week for the next month!

NO PLACE TO HANG DRAPERY RODS

Ideally, drapery rods should be attached to a wood frame for sturdiness. But this isn't always possible, especially if you want to extend your drapes a bit past the window. The chances are you will then find yourself with nothing but Sheetrock to hang them from. And that just won't work. The weight of the drapes will pull the rods off the wall within hours of hanging. My solution is one that would make the average carpenter turn green, but it works, so who cares?

You'll need a piece of scrap wood for each side of the window, two or three inches wide and long enough to reach from the edge of the window trim to the place you want to put the end of the drapery rod. Now, there are bound to be studs (the upright boards inside the wall that support the house frame) next to the window and there may be others a few inches away. These will provide a firm base to attach your board to. What you're going to do is put a good layer of glue on the underside of that piece of wood, then nail it to the wall at the height you plan to put your rod, nailing through the Sheetrock and into that stud next to the window frame and any others you're lucky enough to locate. There's information on how to find studs in the chapter on walls. You'll now have a piece of wood, firmly attached to the wall, that extends from the window molding out to the spot you've marked for your curtain rod. Use plenty of nails so it'll hold, by the way. Now, all you have to do is attach your drapery rod to this piece of wood. Granted, it may be a little rough looking, but you can paint it.

UNSIGHTLY CURTAIN RODS

Want to know how to add a decorator touch to your windows for just the price of a can of spray paint? Here's a little trick I learned from a professional decorator—the way she camouflages those hideous white curtain rods that can ruin the looks of a wood paneled room, or one painted any color but white.

Take the rods down from the wall. Dust them (wash too, if they've accumulated any airborne grease) and lay them out flat on some newspaper. Pick a spot outdoors out of the wind or in a garage or some other place where a bit of spray paint in the air won't hurt anything.

Using a paint which is as near the color of the window molding as possible, spray the rods, being careful not to get too much paint on the cords of traverse rods.

After they're dry, rehang and admire your cleverness. Instead of that ugly slash of white at the top of each window, you'll have a subtle color that blends with the room decor, and is practically invisible. I did this in my wood paneled living room, using a medium brown paint, and you honestly don't even know the rods are there.

BALKY DRAPERY RODS

If a traverse drapery rod will not slide smoothly, just open it all the way and rub paraffin on the track. Slide back and forth a few times and it'll be like new!

WORN VENETIAN BLINDS

Few things are more exasperating than a venetian blind that refuses to work properly. But, you can fix it. When the cord slips and slides around without moving the slats, it usually means the metal casing is so worn that it's lost its grip on the gears and on life. Replacement kits are available from the drapery department of your largest department store. Each brand has its own instructions, clearly printed on the box, and the only tool you'll need to install the blinds is a screwdriver.

To replace a broken or warped slat, leave the blind hanging at the window and loosen the cord from the bottom slat. Slip each succeeding one off until you get to the broken one. Replace it with one from the department store and reverse the process by putting the slats back on and securing the cord at the bottom.

Worn tapes can also be replaced with kits from the drapery department. Again, just follow the directions on the box.

WORN ROLLER SHADES

When the spring in a roller shade has become so loose that the shade won't roll up properly, take it out of the brackets and roll the shade onto the roller by hand. Then, twist the little flat knob that sticks out of one end. You'll feel the spring get tighter. A few good turns should do the trick. Replace it in the brackets.

If it's too tight, you raise it all the way to the top, take it out of the brackets and unroll it by hand about a foot. Replace it in the brackets and see if it doesn't behave then.

A shade that's pulled off the roller can be re-attached with a stapler or tacks.

A badly worn shade can be replaced. Take the shade down from the brackets, remove it from the roller and measure exactly. Ask for this same size at your dime store or department store. (Better still, take the old roller with you.) And, do buy a good quality shade—it'll pay in the long run. Place the roller on the floor, center the new shade and staple or tack it on. Roll it up by hand and replace it in the brackets.

Or if the shade is in pretty fair condition, but is stained or has small holes, you can have some fun and give your windows a shot in the arm at the same time. Holes and tears can be covered with colored plastic tape. Why not use a contrasting color and cut the patches in stars, balloons, flowers, etc.? Ragged edges should be trimmed slightly, then stiffened with a light coat of shellac. Don't use the shade until the shellac is thoroughly dry!

WORN OR FADED AWNINGS

Fabric awnings are bright and colorful when new, but too many of the ones we inherit in older homes leave much to be desired. If yours is in good condition, but faded, you can give the whole place a face lift very easily. Dyeing is one solution, but only works on solid color fabric that is not plastic coated. Just make up a strong liquid dye solution (it covers better if you use the original color), put it in your household sprayer and spray a generous layer all over the fabric.

Striped awnings won't take dye satisfactorily but you can paint them. Select good quality house paint of a color that harmonizes with the house (there may be some left over in the garage!) and mix it about 4 to 1 with thinner (water if you're using latex, turpentine if you have oil paint) so it'll spread easily. If the paint is old and thick, you'll need more thinning agent, naturally. Brush the paint carefully onto the awning fabric, being careful to coat all fibers. Let the paint dry thoroughly (at least one day) before you fold or store the awnings.

Clean your awnings well with a brush and hose before dyeing or painting so the new color can penetrate the fabric successfully.

Don't despair if the old things are leaking like the proverbial sieve every time it rains. That can be fixed, too. If there are no holes, but the fabric is just too porous, mix up a solution of one pound of shaved paraffin in a gallon of turpentine. If the paraffin doesn't melt readily, set the mixing container in a pail of very hot water to speed it up. *DO NOT SET IT ON THE STOVE. IT WILL CATCH FIRE!* Using a big sturdy brush, lather this concoction all over the fabric. The turpentine will evaporate, leaving a thin coat of waterproof paraffin on the fabric. Neat, huh?

Patching is possible, too, for holes of reasonable size. Traditionally, you're supposed to sew the patch on, but it's easier just to glue it. Cut a patch a couple of inches larger than the hole all around, coat all edges (patch and awning) well with epoxy glue, and press firmly together.

Any of these duding-up operations can be performed while the awning is hanging at the window. A professional repairman would undoubtedly take them down, but they're heavy and bulky, so you, a smart woman, will just take the easy way out. Besides, you usually need the awning fabric to be stretched as tightly as possible for dyeing, painting, or patching, and it's stretched tightly on that frame, isn't it? Why not use what's available?

Aluminum awnings seldom need more than an occasional paint job. Use a special paint made for this purpose. Once in a while, though, an aluminum slat will come loose and need to be reset. That's no big problem, though. It was probably put together in the first place with a screw and nut. Check the other slats to be sure. If so, all you have to do is find a screw and nut of the approximate size and screw it back together. If by chance, it was put together with some sort of solder, get a tube of liquid metal and put a healthy dab on each section at the joining place. Hold for a few minutes until the joint begins to set. All done!

PLAIN GLASS WINDOWS WHICH OFFER NO PRIVACY

Do you have a large expanse of glass three feet away from a public sidewalk that has to be kept draped 24 hours a day so you won't feel like a goldfish? Or do you have a bathroom window, eye-level and looking directly into your neighbor's bathroom window, "blessed" with crystal-clear glass? I think any builder or building superintendent who allows such horrors should be shot at sunrise. But that's beside the point. You can block the view very effectively and still allow plenty of light in by frosting the glass with aquarium paint from the local hobby shop. Try out your skill first on some scrap glass (an old wine bottle will do fine) until you can make artistic little swirls with your brush. The effect is delightful!

STATIC ELECTRICITY

If you get shocked every time you open a door knob in cold weather, try covering it with those little knitted coasters. Most static electricity is caused by dry air, accentuated by our furnace burning in winter. A humidifier will correct the situation if you can afford it. Other remedies are: keeping a tea kettle bubbling gently on the stove, using plenty of house plants, and opening the windows a bit when it rains.

3

Furniture

Attractive, Sturdy Furniture Is the
Icing on the Cake of Your Well-Kept Home!

In this country, hundreds of millions of dollars are spent every
year on furniture for homes. Much of this huge sum is spent to
replace old or damaged pieces that could have been salvaged
and made useful with a little well applied knowledge. The
purpose of this chapter is to show you how to successfully
repair and refinish the furniture in your home, thereby saving
money to spend on the really important things, like a week in
Hawaii!

WOBBLY CHAIR AND TABLE LEGS

A wobbly piece of furniture is not only spooky to sit on, it
can be downright dangerous if the whole thing should suddenly
collapse under you one fine day. So, don't put up with that
rickety kitchen chair another minute.

There are two ways to tighten loose table and chair legs. If
you have time and the piece isn't too hard to get apart,
disassemble it completely. Sand the old dried glue away, then
coat each part of each joint with white glue and reassemble. If
there seems to be some play in any of the joints, take one of
your old nylon stockings and place a section of it over the chair
leg or rung before you shove it back into the joint. This should
firm it up. Trim off the excess nylon around the joint with a

razor blade and leave the piece upside down overnight to dry. Don't use it for a day or so.

The quickie method is simply to turn the chair or table upside down and force glue into all the joints. Your white glue must be thinner than when it comes from the bottle to do this, so pour a little into a paper cup and mix a small amount of water with it until it's the consistency of light cream. Dribble this down into the joints and jam wooden toothpicks into any that aren't tight enough to suit you. Leave the piece upside down to dry and harden.

Well-made furniture often has triangular corner braces on the underside. If these become loose, remove them and sand off the old glue. Then coat with fresh glue and reassemble. Some corner braces are reinforced with screws, too. If the screws seem loose when you try to tighten them, jam a couple of wooden toothpicks in the hole, squirt a bit of glue in and try again.

UNEVEN TABLE LEGS

Have you ever tried to cut a table down to a lower height only to find yourself trimming one leg and then another because you never could get them all the same length? I invariably ended up with something that looked as though it was destined for a Japanese tea house until I discovered a little trick. Simply decide how many inches you want to take off and then fill a bucket or large bowl with exactly that many inches of water. Set one leg in the water and mark it at the waterline. Do the same for the other three legs and you'll have a foolproof cutting line on each.

The traditional way to *lengthen* a short table leg is to stick a book of paper matches under it. Now, this really doesn't do much for your decor and you always end up filching the matches anyway, so you're right back where you started. An easy and permanent repair job requires only some plastic wood and a tack. Sand off any paint on the bottom of the leg and stick the tack into it so the head protrudes slightly above the surface. Roll a spoonful of plastic wood into a small ball and press it onto and around the tack, being sure some goes under the head. Then, set the table on a level surface with a piece of wax paper under the repaired leg. The weight of the table will press the plastic wood down to a level with the other legs. If any of it squeegies out too far, cut it away with a knife before it hardens. Then, sand it smooth and finish it to match the rest of the table.

SQUEAKING BEDS

The hardest part about taking the squeak out of a squeaking bed is getting the box spring and mattress off. You have to do that first. Then, for a wooden bed, melt a bit of paraffin over *hot water* (it is highly inflammable and could ignite if melted directly over a flame). Pour the melted paraffin down into all the joints. The wax soaks into the fibers of the wood and forms a lubricant. On a metal bed you squirt lightweight oil into every joint where metal rubs against metal. Rub off any excess because it will stain your box spring.

DRAWERS THAT STICK AND JAM

We've all struggled with sticking drawers at one time or another. This usually happens when the local Tom Jones or your husband's boss is waiting in the living room and you can't get to your contacts or false eyelashes because the darned dresser drawer is jammed. In this case, simply put on your sunglasses, explain casually that you strained your eyes (pick one of the following according to the guest's particular hang-up: a. skiing at Aspen, b. bicycling on the beach in Bermuda, c. researching the curse of King Tutankhamen's tomb at the library, or d. plotting the last eclipse). Then go. You can fix the drawer the next day.

Dampness is usually the culprit when a drawer becomes jammed. If you can get it open a few inches the cure is easy. Borrow a *trouble light* (a light bulb with a wire cage around it on the end of a long cord) from the neighborhood car buff or from your husband's workshop and slip it inside the drawer. The wire keeps the bulb from touching the wooden drawer and scorching it. Turn the light on and let it burn for a couple of hours. The bulb will generate enough heat to dry out the drawer. If this method isn't practical, place a portable heater near the drawer or take the bonnet off your hair dryer, stick the tube in the drawer and turn it on the *low* heat setting.

As soon as the wood has dried out, the drawer can be opened. Now, sand the top and bottom edges of the drawer sides well. Brush on a thin coat of shellac or varnish to seal against the dampness in the future, and when it's dry, coat liberally with paraffin. It shouldn't give you any trouble after that.

Many times this long process isn't necessary. If the drawer will open, but is just balky, try using the paraffin alone.

Drawers will sometimes become worn on old furniture simply through years of use. When this happens you may find that the drawers will work smoothly, closing just fine until they get to the last inch or so. Then, they won't go any farther without lifting. This is because the soft side panels have worn down while the front panel, always of better, harder wood, is still in good condition. An easy way to fix this problem is to press a row of thumbtacks into the track or onto the board that the drawer slides on. This will raise the drawer slightly as it glides in and out and may take care of the condition. If the dresser is *really* old, you might need something with more thickness than a thumbtack. Try tongue depressors, frozen lollipop or sucker sticks, kite sticks, plastic tubing—anything to lift those drawer sides.

LOOSE DRAWER KNOBS

Did you know there's an easy way to tighten a loose dresser or cabinet drawer knob? In the old unimaginative method, you have to unload all the stuff onto the floor so there's room inside the drawer to hold a screwdriver lengthwise.

But, there's a get-it-over-with-in-a-hurry way I like better. All you need is about one inch of free space at the front of the drawer (and if you don't have *that* you need to straighten the drawer anyway!). Just slide the edge of the blade of a table knife down inside the front of the drawer and into the slot in the screw head. Hold it firmly and turn the knob with your other hand. It'll tighten very nicely.

DAMAGED ORNAMENTAL CARVING

Chances are you'll acquire an old carved picture frame some day—via Grandma or that quaint little antique shop you can't resist. These are fantastic decorator accents, but too often bits of the carving will have broken off and disappeared long before you got it. You can replace a piece or two of this fancy work if you have just a bit of skill with your fingers (and you *do* if you can flute a pie crust, make a Christmas wreath, or type more than thirteen words a minute). There is a soft, putty-like, papier-mache substance sold in hobby shops that is very easy to use. You just press a glob of it onto the frame at the damaged spot and shape it like the rest of the carving before it dries. Use your kitchen and beauty tools—spoons, orange stick, serrated cutter, nut pick, etc.—to shape the design. Or you can buy some powdered wood putty at the hardware store, mix it to a thick paste with water, and shape it as needed. This latter substance can be carved and sanded just like wood after it hardens. Don't worry if your patch job doesn't exactly match the original. You'll need to refinish the frame, anyway, and a uniform color will tend to blend the patterns together.

I salvaged an antique mirror and frame once with this trick. It was at an outdoor country auction, where the furnishings of an old resort hotel were being disposed. The auctioneer obviously didn't have much of an eye for salvage because when this mirror came up he snickered and asked if anyone would be willing to bid on it. I'll admit it didn't look like much then. The mirror itself was in perfect condition but the frame was broken completely in half and badly nicked. But, its lovely old carved roses and garlands made me know I had to have it. The rose motif was even repeated on the glass of the mirror, etched in a charming pattern that followed the curving Victorian lines of the frame. I bid $2 and got it. Mine was the only bid. Well, there were some strange looks, as I left, at the crazy woman who'd pay good money for a mirror in three pieces, but those people should see it now! Back home I glued the frame back together with epoxy and built up the broken carving, using the method above. Two coats of soft gold paint later and I had a real gem, one I wouldn't take $100 for now!

Naturally, you can build up any sort of carving with this material, not just frames.

DAMAGE FROM SCRATCHES, DENTS, PAINT, WAX

Minute scratches that don't penetrate the finish itself can be repaired by simply re-waxing. But, don't panic if you discover a *real* scratch. The damage isn't irrevocable and the remedies are right in your own kitchen and bathroom.

On walnut, try rubbing the scratch with the meat of a pecan, walnut, or brazil nut. For mahogany, you'll use a bit of iodine. Apply it with a tiny paint brush (an old mascara or lipstick brush would be perfect) or a toothpick wrapped in cotton. Try not to get any iodine on the rest of the finish and

Fig. 3-1. Touching up a scratch on furniture that has a colored finish by using a matching-colored crayon.

wipe off any excess immediately. If, from advance observation, you think your iodine is darker than the furniture's color, thin it a bit with rubbing alcohol.

You could also use shoe polish, a wax stain, or one of those wax sticks sold in paint stores for this purpose. On furniture with a colored finish, try a child's crayon in a matching shade (Fig. 3-1). Just rub it into the scratch and wipe off the excess. Then, clean the area, apply a coat of wax polish and rub to a sheen.

There is always some clod at every party who manages to park his mint julep on your grandmother's heirloom piano. When you discover the damage the next day, a miserable white ring has formed and you're sick, sick, sick. Obviously, the first thing to do is strike the boor's name from your list. Then, wad a tissue into a ball, dip it in oil and then into one of those overflowing ashtrays that are lying all over the place. Rub the ring gently with this oil/ash mixture and you may be surprised to see it gradually disappear. If this doesn't work (different finishes require different remedies) try table salt, silver polish, or a bit of ammonia on a tissue.

If these fail, there are four more possibilities. But, be sure to test any of them on a hidden spot to make sure they won't damage the finish. In order, try wax and *very* fine steel wool, denatured alcohol, turpentine, or camphorated oil. At least one of these is *bound* to remove that ring!

Candle wax is removed by thoroughly chilling the wax with ice, then picking off as much as you can with your fingernails. Scrape the rest off with a dull knife.

Fresh paint can usually be removed with liquid wax. If it has dried hard, saturate a cotton ball in linseed oil, place on the spot and let it soak for a few hours. You can probably scrape it off then.

Always re-wax after any repair job to your beautiful furniture, naturally!

You know what a dent is, of course. It's that miserable little hole left where you dropped that five pound cast iron incense burner on the coffee table. But, according to the experts, a dent is an area where wood fibers have been compressed through pressure. In order to get rid of the dent, you must un-compress those fibers. Heat and steam will usually do it by making the fibers swell back to their original level.

To allow the steam to penentrate the wood, you must first remove all wax and polish with turpentine. This won't hurt the finish. Just rub the area around the dent gently with a soaked rag or piece of cotton, then remove any excess turpentine with a dry tissue. Fold a piece of cheesecloth or other soft loosely woven fabric into a tiny pad, dampen thoroughly with water and place over the dent. Allow this to sit for an hour or two, renewing the water if the pad begins to dry out. Place a metal bottle cap, flat side down, on the damp pad directly over the dent. Set your iron to "high" and place it on the cap. The heat will be transferred through the bottle cap, create steam from the wet pad and should swell the dented fibers. If the first attempt isn't successful, try again. It may take several applications. Then, wax and polish.

BLISTERED VENEER

Veneered furniture is made by gluing a thin layer of expensive cabinet wood to a base of cheaper wood. The glue between these layers can be loosened if moisture from flower pots, vases, etc., comes in contact with the veneer for extended periods. This can happen even if you put a plate or tile under the damp base because condensation often forms under the plate. You'll know the glue has lost its hold on life when you see a blister forming and little cracks appearing on the wood's finish. As usual, there are two acceptable ways to correct this. The simplest is to cover the area with a piece of heavy brown grocery bag paper and literally iron the blister down with your ordinary laundry iron. Set the heat at a medium setting and don't use any steam. Use pressure and go over the area two or three times. Then, immediately lift the paper and rub a cold flat surface (heavy skillet, jar of cold cream, etc.) over the area you've just heated. What you've done is soften the old glue through heat and then hardened it again by the sudden cooling.

The other method is to take a razor blade and carefully slit the blister. Cut *with* the grain of the wood and it won't show later. Lay a damp cloth over the blister until the wood is slightly soft, then press one side down and push some white glue into the other side with a knife. Then, press that side down and insert glue under the other side of the blister. Wipe off any excess glue and put a weight on the area to hold it until the glue has set.

Either way you're probably going to have to refinish the whole piece in order to have a table, television set, or what-have-you that is a complement to your room.

FURNITURE IN NEED OF COMPLETE REFINISHING

If a piece of furniture is too badly damaged for spot repair or if you're just plain tired of looking at that bilious blond end table you picked up at a neighborhood garage sale, then you'll want to try a complete refinishing job. This can be loads of fun—a real hobby, in fact—and quite satisfying to your creative instincts. But before you start, make an honest evaluation of the piece of furniture in question.

Is it good solid cabinet wood such as mahogany, walnut, cherry, etc.? If so, then it will be well worth your time and elbow grease to try a really professional job of restoration. Otherwise you'd be better off, and end up with a more handsome piece of furniture, to consider antiquing.

There are two preliminary steps to restoring a fine piece of furniture. The first involves completely removing all traces of the old finish. Professionals often *scrape* away the old finish. They use a specially made hook-type scraper which literally *peels* the old finish off right down to the bare wood. You can use this tool, too, if you have the strength and if the piece is a flat surface.

By far the easier way to remove old paint and varnish, though, is with a semi-paste chemical remover. This is a highly potent concoction you get in the paint department. Most brands are inflammable and you must never smoke, or allow anyone around to do so, while you're using it. If at all possible, work out of doors. If you can't, keep the windows open and lay a thick pad of newspapers under the work to catch drips, or you're liable to take the finish off all the furniture for three floors down.

Wearing rubber gloves, simply spread this paste thickly on the piece, wait a few minutes (the can will tell you how long) until the old finish has wrinkled up into a hideous mess that looks like a night-roaming swamp creature out of the late, late horror movies. Then, scrape the goo off with a rag. Some kinds require a final wiping with turpentine, others need a water rinse. You will probably have to repeat the process in any deep grooves or carvings. I've found that an old toothbrush helps to rout out the last bits of goo and finish in those crevices.

It's much easier to remove a plain shellac finish. Just wipe thoroughly with a rag soaked with alcohol and let dry (Fig. 3-2).

After the old finish is off, you begin sanding. Although electric sanders are great for some jobs, I wouldn't recommend them for use on a good piece of furniture. They remove material at a fantastic rate, and it's too easy to dig a hole where you only intended to brush the surface.

Sandpaper is available in degrees all the way from a grade that looks as though you could resurface the driveway with it to the finest garnet paper. Avoid, let me repeat, *avoid*, the

Fig. 3-2. Removing plain shellac finish by wiping with a rag soaked in alcohol.

Gravel Gertie stuff. It's rough enough to scratch a pawnbroker's heart. Get a few sheets of the finest grade and a couple that are just a bit coarser.

The easiest way to sand down flat surfaces such as tabletops is with a sanding block. This is just a block of scrap wood of a size to fit comfortably in your hand, say three inches wide, six inches long, and two inches deep. Pad it along one long side with felt or several thicknesses of rags. Tear a rectangle of sandpaper (easily done by creasing it at the desired line, placing on the edge of the table and tearing down the crease) about two inches wider and two inches longer than your block, and place it over the padding. Bend the excess around the block and tack or staple to the sides. This gives you an easy-to-use tool that can be thrown away when the job is done. If the wood block is too hard to locate, just forget it and wrap the sandpaper around your fingers.

Sand *with* the grain of the wood, gently at first until you can gauge how fast the work is going, then gradually increase your pressure and speed. For edgings and ornate areas, tear off pieces of sandpaper just big enough to hold around your finger tips. Sometimes an emery board will reach into crevices when nothing else will. A good way to sand round table legs is with long strips of sandpaper worked in a "shoeshine" motion.

I've found it easier to sand rough, porous wood if you give it a coat of one-half shellac and one-half denatured alcohol first. Allow the piece to dry for about an hour before sanding.

Your fingertips will tell you when you're through: run them lightly over the surface and when they detect no tiny scratches, no invisible nicks, no stubborn patches of old finish, you're ready to go on.

The finish you apply, the second big step in refinishing, will be determined by the wood itself, to a large extent. Oak and mahogany always require a preliminary sealer. This is a clear liquid which is brushed onto the raw wood to seal the fibers and prevent blotching. Sealer does not color the wood, and you'll want to follow it with an oil stain which will.

Oil stains are available to give the effect of walnut, fruitwood, mahogany, or almost any other fine wood. Even wood of a very poor color can be transformed into instant beauty with stain. Staining is also in order when you have five different kinds of wood in your living room and would like to get rid of the "early attic" effect.

Stains are brushed on, left a few minutes, and then wiped off with a rag. The longer the stain is left on the wood, the darker its final color will be. So, be careful! Stains actually dye the wood and once applied aren't easy to remove. It's a good idea to experiment on a hidden spot first so you don't end up with black walnut when what you wanted was light pecan!

Staining is not a final finish. You must protect the wood and the stain with at least two coats of varnish. For most furniture, use satin finish varnish. This is low luster and gives a quality hand-rubbed look. However, when you're working with a piece of furniture which will be subjected to heat or water, use spar varnish. This is a waterproof, exterior grade and has a high gloss. Regardless of the type of varnish you use, always sand very lightly between coats and dust thoroughly before going on.

Waxing then gives a final, quality touch.

Liquid sealer can also be used to give a quick "oiled" or "waxed" effect to wood such as walnut which has a good natural color. This eliminates both the staining and varnishing processes. The traditional cabinetmaker's method was to apply layer after layer of linseed oil, and rub long and lovingly in between. This could take *weeks*. But, you can get virtually the same effect by applying a few coats of liquid sealer. The luster is soft and glowing and quite lovely when finished off with a thin coat of paste wax.

Some pieces of furniture simply don't warrant all that work, however, Either the wood is of poor quality or it's so badly banged up that no amount of effort could make it rival a new, expensive piece. So, don't try. You can still salvage *any* piece of furniture that's sturdy, though, and from it make a decorative, useful addition to your home. Antiquing is the secret. And, on an antiqued piece, those nicks and deep scratches you can't hide often add to the character of the old thing.

I have a friend who wrapped up the antiquing craze with this observation: "Antiquing is when you take something in pretty good shape and then spend all day making it look old!" True, true. But it's a whale of a lot of fun and a great way to disguise and coordinate a houseful of thrift shop bargains, your kitchen cabinets, a door, or even a whole wall!

Actually, antiquing is a very old technique and you can see some beautiful examples (circa Marie Antoinette) in the museums today. Those old cabinetmakers had to put in many months of hard work, though, to get the same effect (well, almost) that you can produce today in a few hours with a kit. These kits are available in a rainbow of colors for about $5 each at most paint stores. They also come in wood tones that would fool a woodpecker.

Before you begin, take a good long look at any piece of furniture you plan to antique, especially if it was made during the early part of this century. If it's a buffet, for example, the chances are there is a tacky little curved backboard nailed onto the top and it has long spindly legs that only a flamingo could love. Lop off the backboard, cut the legs down or replace them with short ones, and you'll have the makings for a very handsome lowboy. Most ornamentation is only tacked on and adds little to the style. Whack it off! It's amazing what good lines some second-hand gems have when you get rid of the gingerbread.

Remove all hardware that doesn't require dismantling the thing. That means drawer knobs and pulls, mainly. Most do-it-yourself manuals demand that you take *all* hardware off. But, you're the one who has to put those hinges back on, not them. So, unless the hinges are solid brass and really beautiful, just slap the base coat right over the whole shebang.

Antiquing will cover many sins of the past, but you'll have a better job if you can do away with some before you start. Fill holes with wood putty and sand down the nicks and scratches.

Clean the piece with solvent or soap and water. You must remove all traces of old wax, grime, and dust or your pretty new finish won't stick. Check and repair loose legs, sticking drawers, and wobbly doors. Then, you're ready for the fun part.

The base coat is an opaque paint that conceals the old finish completely. Brush it on and let it dry. Some kits require overnight drying, others are ready for the second coat within an hour or so. If your piece has lovely moldings or panels you want to accentuate, brush a coat of contrasting color and gold paint on them with an artist's brush after the base coat is dry.

The glaze is a brownish overcoat that gives the "old" look. Apply over the base coat with a brush and let set for a few minutes. Then wad up some cheesecloth and begin wiping the glaze away, turning the cloth as it gets full. Discard it when it's saturated and get another. Work from one far edge to the other; never start or stop in the middle of a surface as this will ruin the grain. Genuinely old furniture is usually darker in

44

crevices, around hinges, and in corners. You can get the same effect by allowing more glaze to remain on at those spots. Just don't wipe so hard.

Most of the kits say you don't need a final finish, but I've found it pays to protect that little beauty you've just created with a coat of low-luster varnish. Accidents do happen, and it's practically impossible to go back and make an undetectable repair to an antiqued surface.

QUICKIE TIPS

Want to know an easy way to paint those pesky drawer knobs? Just set the knob, with its screw in place, in the top of a non-returnable pop bottle, then spray it (Fig. 3-3). Clever? No missed spots, no finger marks, and no painted fingers!

You can't stick a picture frame in a pop bottle but here's a trick that's just as good: Find a piece of thin scrap wood that's longer than the picture frame is wide. A wooden yardstick is perfect. Tack the stick to the back of the frame, catching it on both sides of the frame and letting it extend at least a foot on one side. What do you now have, friend? A picture frame with a handle! Just hold the handle and paint to your heart's

Fig. 3-3. Spray-painting doorknobs by placing them, screw-down, in soda bottles.

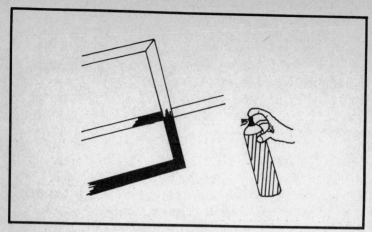

Fig. 3-4. Spray-painting frames by devising a makeshift handle.

content (Fig. 3-4). You can twist and turn your frame anyway you like, doing a much better job than by setting it down on a sheet of newspaper. After the frame is dry it's easy to pull the handle away, with no damage done to your lovely frame.

Need a really elegant antique picture frame but don't have the price of admission? Do what a clever friend of mine did. She went to the dime store and found an inexpensive composition frame which had fairly decent carving but which was painted a hideous flat white with cheap gold trim. By using up the last of an antiquing kit, left over from her last creative binge, she transformed it into an almost genuine antique mahogany heirloom—perfect to frame her prize needlepoint.

4

Floors

They're Always Underfoot!

Got the dismal-floor blahs? Cheer up—if what's underfoot is ruining the looks of your place, you can spruce the floors up with just a little effort, and not much cash.

WORN LINOLEUM

The new vinyl floorcoverings are not very expensive, and if you live in your own home, you will probably want to simply replace old, worn linoleum with either tiles or roll-type floorcovering.

If money is tight or if you're renting, though, it's a different story. Assuming the landlord will let you (and he will if you explain confidently that you're getting to be a real *expert* on this home repair thing and you're undoubtedly going to add at least a month's rent in value to his place), there are several ways to spruce up dreary floorcoverings.

Linoleum often develops badly worn areas at doorways, in front of the sink, etc., even when the rest of the floor is in reasonably good condition. If you can dig up some scraps left over from the original installation, you can actually *patch* it, and in no more time than it takes to patch the jeans you ripped on that last rock climb.

Cut an evenly shaped piece from the scrap, a little larger than the worn area, and lay it directly over the damaged spot. With a *sharp* single-edged razor blade cut through the old linoleum, using the patch as a guide. Pry the old linoleum out, and the patch will perfectly into the hole. Before you slip it in, though, coat the underside of the patch with linoleum cement if you can get a bit. It comes in large cans and you may not want to invest that much, though. If not, use a good quality waterproof contact cement.

Fit the patch in and smooth it down with your hands. If it shows a tendency to lift a bit around the edges, put a layer of waxed paper over the whole patch and weight it down with heavy books for a few hours.

Unless you're a lot better of a linoleum-fixer than I am, you'll find there's a tiny crack showing all around the patch. Don't worry, this is fixable, too. Locate a child's crayon the same color as the linoleum and melt it down over low heat. While the wax is still molten, pour it into the crack and press in with your fingers. Scrape off any that spills over onto the floor. Now, clean, wax, and buff your floor and believe me—it would take a Sherlock Holmes to discover the repair!

The same ploy (the crayon bit) can be used to fill small cracks or holes that don't merit a patch.

But what if you have no scraps, or the whole thing is on its last legs? Well, you can still get a little more wear out of the old horror by simply painting it with a good floor and deck enamel. Be sure to remove every trace of wax and dirt first with solvent, then soap and water.

Admittedly, a painted floor is pretty dull, even one that's covered with Fascinating Fuchsia, but, you can give it some zip by "spattering" on a confetti pattern with leftover paint of other colors. Just dip an old toothbrush in paint, then draw it rapidly across a comb or piece of screen wire to make it spatter onto the floor. Use several colors for a really gay effect. But, practice on some newspaper in the backyard first to develop your technique!

Or, dream up your own idea for a unique pattern. One of the cutest bathrooms I ever saw was a tiny cubicle in a rented apartment. The clever girl who lived there had painted the whole thing—walls, ceilings, and floor linoleum—with white enamel. After it was dry, she'd gone back and added an elegant pattern by dipping a natural sponge lightly in gold paint and pressing it onto the enamel—the ceiling, too!—in a random pattern. With gold shower curtains, rug, and towels, it was right out of a sultan's harem.

Are you the uninhibited type? Then, paint red, white, and blue stripes, silver stars, foot-wide checks, or even a fake persian rug (complete with fringe), on the base coat. Use pie pans, masking tape, tools, *anything* for patterns. Wild!

LINOLEUM THAT'S LOST ITS GRIP ON LIFE

Sometimes the adhesive under old linoleum will dry out and a bulge will result. You can fix this in less than an hour. If the bulge is near a seam, pry the linoleum up at the seam and poke linoleum cement under it with a spatula or putty knife, making sure you get the cement into the edges of the bulge.

If the bulge is in the center of the floor, take a sharp razor blade and slit the linoleum through the bulge, poke in some linoleum cement, and spread it out to the edges of the bulge.

In either case, clean off any cement that oozed out on top and weight the repair down until it dries.

LAYING VINYL OR CARPET TILE

You may want to do a bang-up job of refurbishing the floor someday by covering it with new tile or those delicious carpet tiles. They're simple to put down, and you can do a room between breakfast and lunch—if you have an early breakfast. Get the kind with the peel-off backing. They're a little more expensive than the kind you lay with mastic, but they're so much simpler to use that it's worth the few extra dollars.

I only have two words of wisdom for you. First, don't attempt to lay tile on a floor in really poor condition. By that I mean one that's so uneven you can see ridges or one that sags badly in a corner or two. You'd just be wasting your money. You need a good base for the results to be professional-looking.

Second, always start in the dead center of the room. It will seem easier and more natural to start in a corner, but this can lead to trouble when you get to the opposite corner. Few, if any, rooms are perfectly square, but those tiles are. In fact, it isn't at all unusual for a room to be "out of square" (that means crooked) by several inches. If you start in a corner, and lay those square tiles, one after the other across the room, you're liable to find yourself with a weird pie-shaped angle to fill on the other side. And, all the way across the room, the lines between the tiles may be slightly out of kilter. Years of looking at those lines on the bias could drive you to drink!

To find the center, draw diagonal lines from corner to corner of the room and begin laying the tile where they intersect. Line the first tile up parallel with a side wall and go on from there.

REFINISHING HARDWOOD FLOORS

A softly gleaming oak floor is a thing of beauty, and proof positive (in your house) to that visiting ex-college roommate that you really do have some smarts buried under that curly mop. So she made Phi Beta Kappa and you barely squeaked through? Bet she doesn't know how to keep a floor like that, and you're about to learn! The finish on a hardwood floor that isn't badly abused can be renewed several times before *complete* refinishing is necessary.

First, remove the old, dirty wax with mineral spirits. *DO THIS ON A DAY YOU CAN KEEP THE WINDOWS OPEN! THE VAPORS ARE NOXIOUS AND INFLAMMABLE!* Work quickly, wiping up the solvent and old wax as you go along, before it can dry and resettle on the floor. You may run into spots of thick, resistant wax. If so, use a little steel wool (plain, not the soap-filled pads) to loosen them. Now, take a good look at the floor. If the finish appears to be in good condition all you need to do is apply another fresh coat of paste wax and buff it (with a rented mechanical buffer) to a sheen.

You may run into worn, damaged areas, around doorways especially. Spot repair is sometimes all that's necessary. Just clean as above, then sand the worn spot gently with a fine-grained sandpaper to remove roughness and any gloss left over from the original finish.

Apply a penetrating sealer to the sanded area, let it dry, then varnish with good quality clear varnish. Now, re-wax, buff, and admire your beautiful new floor!

If you inherit a floor which is so far gone that it's beyond these stopgap repair methods, it needs complete refinishing. Sand it down to the bare wood and, seal it, fill it, varnish it, and wax it just as though it were brand new. This can be done, and the results are gorgeous, but that sanding is a little tricky and I'd advise you to have a professional do it. He'll use a mechanical sander, which removes the top layer of your floor with lightning speed. It takes practice to know how to sand just enough without gouging out big indentations in the floor, and I'd hate for you to ruin your floor while you learn!

REMOVING MARKS FROM FLOORS AND CARPETING

Somehow, floors and carpeting have an uncanny ability to attract stubborn marks—but there are always cures:

Hardwood Floors

For most *stains* and *marks* on hardwood floors, just rub *very* lightly with unsoaped fine-grain steel wool. Then, clean with a cloth dampened with vinegar, turpentine, or mineral spirits. Let stand a few minutes, then wipe dry. Repeat if necessary. Fine sandpaper may be used instead of the steel wool if the mark is stubborn. Apply a thin coat of paste wax and buff to a sheen.

Deep stains require a little more drastic action. Sand the damaged area lightly, then apply ordinary household bleach. You'll want to wear rubber gloves to protect your fingers. Apply the bleach carefully to *only* the stained area, using a damp cloth. Let the bleach penetrate a few minutes, then wipe it off with several applications of a damp cloth. You'll need to refinish the area to match the rest of the floor. (See the earlier paragraphs on refinishing hardwood floors.)

Faint scratches can be removed by waxing and buffing. *Deep scratches* may need some color rubbed into the raw wood to blend it with the rest of the floor. Look for colored wax touch-up sticks at the lumber company or a touch-up polish from a good furniture department. Be sure the color you get is as close as possible to the floor's color. Then, follow through with waxing and buffing.

Small dents can be raised by using the bottle cap method explained in the chapter on furniture. For really *large indentations*, place a damp towel over the damage, and press a hot iron against the towel until the wood fibers expand. You'll need to sand the floor very lightly to smooth the fibers, then rewax and buff.

Vinyl, Asbestos, and Linoleum

These hard surfaces are pretty impervious to staining, and almost any marks will remain on the surface instead of soaking down into the material itself. You only have to get it off that surface.

Try using polishing wax. Or a bit of household cleanser. If that won't work, use very fine steel wool, but please don't bear down too hard! You could rub right through that lovely never-needs-waxing finish.

Carpeting

Ah, love that wall-to-wall shag carpet! And, since you can easily spend a month's salary on one small room of good quality carpet, it pays to know how to handle those inevitable mistakes that you, your children, your friends, or the dog will make.

For most stains follow this general procedure:

1. Remove as much of the potential stain as possible by sponging up liquids with a white cloth. Semi-solids should be scraped off with a spoon or spatula.

2. Apply a quality dry-cleaning fluid with a white cloth, blotting gently and working from the edges of the spot toward the center.

3. Follow with a gentle rug-cleaning solution (most of the commercial ones sold in the grocery store are fine), blotting, again, from the edges of the spot toward the center. Absorb excess water with a clean cloth.

4. Let the carpet dry quickly. You can speed the process by turning a fan or your hair dryer onto the damp area. If you accidentally get the rug *very* wet (shame!), place a layer of terry towels over the damp spot and weight them down with something heavy that will absorb the excess moisture.

5. If the stain is still visible, repeat steps two and three.

6. Again, dry the carpet and brush the pile gently with a household brush and restore the nap and texture.

Of course, use your good sense, too. If you *know* the stain is of a type easily removed with detergent and water (coffee, blood, water-based paint, etc.) then skip the cleaning fluid and concentrate on step three.

You didn't! You did. You spilled iridescent pink nail polish on your beautiful white rug—and it's sitting there, screaming at you to *do something!* With luck, your rug is *not* made of acetate fibers, because if it is, you're out of luck. Only a professional can treat nail polish stains on acetate, and often he can't repair the damage.

However, even a butterfingers who can't hold onto a bottle of polish can take nail polish from wool, nylon, polyester, or any of a dozen other rug fibers. If the polish is still wet, absorb as much as possible on a dry cloth. *Do not spread the stain around!* If the stain has hardened, get an eyedropper and drop ordinary nail polish remover onto the stain, drop by drop, letting it slowly penetrate the hardened mass. Lacking an eyedropper, use the tip of a spoon. Keep at it until the polish is soft again.

Scrape off as much of the soft polish as possible using a spoon with a dull edge. Then, begin swabbing polish remover onto the stain, turning and changing the cloth frequently. Repeat the mopping until every trace of polish is gone. Then, do your nails in the bathroom or at the kitchen cabinet after this!

Incidentally, nail polish remover will also take out ball point ink stains.

I don't like to sound so negative, but if you've *burned* your carpet with a cigarette, you're due for a slap on the hand, because it's damaged for good. If you've been living right, though, maybe the burn is just on the tip of the fibers. In that case, just carefully clip off the blackened ends of the tufts using your manicure scissors. Then, suds the area lightly with that rug shampoo we mentioned at the beginning of the section.

It's very difficult for a do-it-yourselfer to remove rust stains from carpet at home. and it's dangerous, too, because the chemicals necessary to rub out the ugly red stain are potent and need the know-how of a professional. However, if you discover a *fresh* rust stain, try the general cleaning method provided at the beginning of this section. It could work.

Besides the companionship it gives so freely, a good dog is a sensible possession for a woman living alone. But, those big loyal shepherds and elegant poodles all start life as puppies. And, puppies are not known for their good manners.

Animal stains can usually be removed if treated *promptly*. Sponge the spot with several applications of clean, lukewarm water. Mop up the water with a clean cloth. Then, apply a generous solution of the following: 1 part white vinegar to one part lukewarm water. Allow this to dry, then use the general cleaning method mentioned early in this chapter. When it is dry, reapply the vinegar solution, and allow it to remain on the area for fifteen minutes or so. Then, begin sponging the area with a cloth dampened in lukewarm water. This treatment is usually effective.

MISCELLANEOUS CARPET PROBLEMS

Carpets can come up with all sorts of problems. Here are some solutions:

Crushed Nap

Some carpet fibers will spring right back after being crushed under a heavy piece of furniture. Others lie there looking completely defeated by life. You can restore their life and vitality by simply brushing the pile up with a stiff, dampened brush. Shag carpeting will respond to loving care with a rug rake, a funny little gadget that looks like a garden tool for leprechauns. Just pull it through the long fibers to restore the shaggy look.

Static Electricity

There are anti-static agents on the market which will help to reduce that unpleasant shock treatment you often get when touching a door knob after walking across the carpet. Better consult a carpet dealer though before buying one. Some have unpleasant side effects such as attracting dirt.

The time-honored method is simply to introduce more humidity into your home. Place pans of water on radiators in the winter (this is when you'll notice the static electricity most). Or keep a kettle of water boiling gently on the stove. Commercial humidifiers also do an excellent job. If you have a *real* problem with static electricity, and own your own home, you might consider having a humidifier installed on your furnace. This will cost about $100 depending upon the size of your home and the price that labor for installation gets in your town. You renters can buy space humidifers which do a fine job, require no installation, and can be taken with you when you get the wanderlust again.

Worn Rug

Custom designed rugs are out of sight, pricewise. But, I have a clever friend who made her own from a worn out living room rug! She bought a dozen discontinued carpet samples for 25¢ each from the local department store, and rolls of carpet tape. Then, using a round platter for a guide, she cut circles out of the carpet wherever it showed wear. Using the same platter as a pattern she cut circles from the *samples*, then she flipped the rug over on its face and fitted the sample circles, face side down, into the holes in the rug. Each circle was secured in its hole with several strips of the carpet tape.

Right side up again, she suddenly had a "custom" carpet as decorative as a Mondrian painting. You should see the attention it gets at parties! I've seen people spend the whole evening crawling around on their hands and knees feeling the carpet!

Worn Carpet on Staircases

The edges of the steps on staircases always take a beating, and carpet here will wear out years before that in the rest of the house.

Frayed carpeting would make even the grand staircase in Buckingham Palace look shabby, and I'll bet (pure guesswork, based on feminine intuition) the thrifty British housekeepers of that historic manse have used this simple little trick at least *once* to keep the old barn presentable: All you have to do is take the carpet off the steps—it's just tacked on—and move it *uphill* a few inches, the distance of the width of the step. This will put the worn part out of sight, on the joints between steps and risers, and expose a completely fresh section of carpet to the edges of the steps. Cut the carpet on that uppermost frayed line and tack it down again.

Now, this is going to leave you with a bare riser at the bottom of the staircase. You can use the piece you cut off from the top to patch it, a scrap from the original installation if you can find one, or a matching carpet sample from the carpet store. The whole process shouldn't take more than one evening of easy work and you'll really give the old pad a shot in the arm.

If you should ever decide to have the staircase re-carpeted, *insist* that the installers figure on an extra foot in length. Then, have them turn *under* that surplus at the top. It'll just make the top step a little bouncier. Then, every couple of years, *before the carpet starts to wear*, take the carpet off and move it downhill an inch or so, releasing a bit of the turned under carpet to fill in at the top.

This way, your carpet will stay fresh and pretty with no visible wear for many, many years longer than it would ordinarily. And, you can pat yourself on the back for being such a smart cookie!

5

Walls

They're All Around Us!

I ran across a quotation not long ago about walls: "Whatever you have in your rooms, think first of the walls, for they are what make your house and home, and if you do not make sacrifices in their favor you will find your chambers have a kind of makeshift, lodging-house look, however rich and handsome your movables may be."

This little gem of wisdom was written for the elegant homes of a hundred years ago, but it applies to today's buffet apartment or ranch-style home just as much as it did to those twenty-room mansions. Keep those walls attractively decorated—and be it ever so humble, your home will be a source of pride and joy.

HOW TO HANG ALMOST
ANYTHING ONTO ALMOST ANYTHING

Breathes there a woman with soul so dead who never to herself has said, "I can't stand that bare wall another minute!" A dull expanse of paint simply screams at us to cover it with pictures, bookcases, needlework, or wagon wheels.

It behooves you to know several different ways to hang things because we run into some pretty weird situations sometimes. You should see the way I have the mirror over my piano anchored to the wall! I bought the mirror at a church garage sale, and it is undoubtedly the heaviest and most beautiful $4' \times 5'$ mirror in existence. After I finished re-vamping it I put the traditional screw eyes on the back and strung it with extra heavy duty picture wire. I picked it up by the wire for testing—and the wire broke. Back I hied myself to the hardware store for more wire. This time I bought some that looked strong enough to support the Golden Gate Bridge. I doubled it and twisted it and rewired my treasure. It broke, too. (I told you the mirror was heavy!)

That evening a friend and I were at the Little Bear, our local beer and country music bistro. Behind the bandstand is a mirror I've coveted ever since I moved to this village. It must be ten feet tall and six feet wide—all encased in an ornate gilded frame. Suddenly I actually *looked* at it for the first time. How on earth was the thing hung? If they could hang that gargantuan beauty, I could certainly hang mine. When the band left for a break I investigated and discovered it was *chained* to the wall and resting on the floor.

Well, to make a long story short, I bought two extra large screw eyes (about 4 inches long), and three heavy brackets. I screwed the brackets to the wall at the place I wanted the lower edge of the mirror to rest, then screwed the screw eyes into the studs about three feet above the brackets. I got a handful of heavy "S" hooks and with the help of my friend, wrestled that mirror up onto the brackets. While I held it steady, he slipped the S hooks through the screw eyes on the wall and then through the ones on the back of the mirror. Voila! Magnifico! And all that. It absolutely makes the room—and there is no *way* that mirror will fall unless the whole house goes first.

That is a little far out, I'll admit, but I just mentioned it to show you that you *can* hang absolutely anything you take a notion to, if you use the right hanger and a little imagination.

HANGERS

Everything depends upon the object you're hanging and the surface from which you want to hang it. Just remember, no *hanger* is any stronger than the wall to which it's attached. You simply can't hang a bookcase loaded with 1000 pounds of books to a Sheetrock wall. *But*, there are studs behind that Sheetrock—reliable boards that are strong enough to serve as the framework for the house—and *they* will support that bookcase. All you have to do is get your hangers anchored into them. On the other hand, a towel bar for the bathroom requires very little support. So, it behooves you to know about several different types of hangers.

Molly Bolts

Molly bolts are great for attaching moderate weight objects (the average dresser mirror, etc.) to Sheetrock walls (and this includes walls covered with thin wood paneling, too). The technical name for Molly bolts is "hollow-wall fasteners," but everyone knows them as Molly bolts, so ask for that. This hanger is a slotted cylinder of thin metal with a screw inside it. You drill a hole in the wall (or ram your screwdriver through if you have one about the same size as the Molly bolt), insert the bolt, then tighten the screw until you feel it begin to take hold behind the wall. What has happened is that those slots have expanded behind the Sheetrock and flared out to form a sturdy anchor. Back the screw out all the way (the Molly bolt will stay in the wall), run the screw through the hanging hole of whatever you're hanging, put it back into the Molly bolt, and tighten once again with your screwdriver.

The one big disadvantage with Molly bolts is that once they're in the wall, they're in to stay. You can't remove them without cutting a larger hole in the wall. However I've *camouflaged* many a useless Molly bolt by removing the screw, covering the little metal flange and the hole with Spackle, then painting over. It's completely invisible.

Toggle Bolts

Toggle bolts will support heavier loads than Molly bolts (but not that 1000-pound bookcase, yet!). A toggle bolt is a long, thin bolt with a pair of spring-operated "wings" on it. The general operation is much the same as that of Molly bolts except that you remove the bolt from the wings first, insert the bolt through the object to be hung, put the wings back on and, holding them in a folded position, push them through the hole you've drilled in the wall. Then, you begin turning the bolt with your screwdriver. The wings will have flared out behind the Sheetrock and will be forced up against it as you tighten the bolt, gripping the wall. Toggle bolts are fine for most shelving, cabinets, etc.

Nylon Anchors

Nylon anchors are great for attaching towel bars, lightweight curtain rods, etc., to Sheetrock walls. Even though these objects are not heavy, you can't just put a nail or screw in the wall to hold them. They will eventually pull out of the Sheetrock.

The nylon anchor has a screw inserted into a small hard nylon casing which is split down the sides. You drill the appropriate size hole, and insert the casing. Put the screw through the object to be hung and into the casing. As you tighten the screw the casing expands, gripping the Sheetrock.

Picture Hangers

Conventional picture hangers are good for hanging things *on* the wall, not attaching things *to* the wall. These are the hangers you've seen at the dime store—just shiny metal hooks. They attach to the walls with a small nail which is inserted through the hanger and into the wall at an angle. It's this angle which supports the weight of your picture or small mirror without pulling out of the wall. Picture hangers come in several sizes for different weights, and two of the largest size will hold up most pictures. If you're hanging that picture on plaster put a piece of transparent tape on the wall before you drive the nail in. It keeps it from cracking the plaster.

Gummed Cloth Hanger

Gummed cloth hangers are small rectangles of white fabric, gummed on the back, with a little chrome hook attached to a flap on the front. They will support any lightweight picture or plaque. Their big advantage is that they require *no nail* and can be removed by moistening with warm water. If your lease says "no nails in the walls!"—this is what to use.

Concrete Screw Anchors

Don't despair because you're stuck with a concrete block wall. It's a little harder to deal with, but you can cover it with your treasures just as well as your friend down the street who lucked out with wood or Sheetrock walls.

The essential tool you'll need is an electric drill with a masonry bit. This is a bit which is especially hardened to be able to make holes in concrete.

Ask for some *screw anchors* at the hardware store, plus the ordinary wood screws to fit into them. Back home, mark the places on the wall, and drill holes to fit the screw anchors (check in advance to make sure your masonry bit will drill holes the size of the anchors). Place an anchor in each hole and drive the wood screws into it just as though you were working with a wood wall.

LOCATING STUDS

Now, to get back to that half-ton bookcase...

It, and almost anything else, can be hung, even from a Sheetrock-covered wall, if you locate the studs, and fasten a sturdy enough hanger into those studs.

First, though, for those of you who aren't too sure what we're talking about: *studs* are vertical lengths of wood used in the framework of the house. They lie between the outside surface and the interior surface. They are usually 3 3/4 inches wide and 1 1/2 inches thick. They are placed in the wall with the 1 1/2 inch thickness at right angles to the interior surfacing. In other words, as you stand there staring at that expanse of wall, there will be a series of places where 1 1/2 inches of good solid wood lies waiting for your use! The trick lies in locating those places.

Studs are usually placed every 16 inches along a wall. Occasionally, a carpenter will set them every 24 inches apart, but this doesn't happen often and is not considered good construction.

The crudest, but still most effective, means of locating a stud is by simply tapping your knuckles along the wall. It works best for me if I close my eyes, for some reason. Rap smartly at a corner. It should give a solid "thud," because there is always a stud at every corner. Now move your knuckles a few inches and rap again. The sound should be a little different—slightly hollow. There is no stud there. If your sense of hearing is acute, you can locate studs this way. To help, measure sixteen inches from the corner and make a tiny mark on the wall, then continue measuring and marking every 16 inches until you get to the approximate spot you want to use. This should give you a pretty good idea of where the stud is. This measuring doesn't always work, though, because the carpenter may have had to alter his placement of the boards for windows, doors, or other construction items, or he may simply have been a sloppy carpenter. (They *do* exist, believe me.)

Some do-it-yourselfers determine the placement of studs by a combination of measuring, thumping, and then drilling tiny holes near the baseboard. They then trace a line straight up from the hole (if they hit a stud, that is) and figure on there being a stud there. There isn't anything wrong with this if you don't mind having a lot of holes drilled into your wall and if the board happens to be perfectly straight. Lots of them aren't, unfortunately. So much "green" (uncured and damp) lumber is used in homes today that many boards warp completely out of line after they're installed.

Or, you can buy a stud finder from the hardware store. This is a device that works by magnetism. You move it slowly along the wall and it will be attracted to the nails inside the wall (therefore, to the studs holding those nails). This is a fair method, not foolproof. I'm partial to the thump-and-listen means of locating.

Once you've located the studs and marked them, drill holes through the Sheetrock or paneling deep enough to pierce the stud by about 1 inch. You can figure on about a 3/4 inch thickness for Sheetrock and 1/4 inch for most paneling. So, in most cases you need to drill a hole at least two inches deep. One way to make sure the hole is deep enough is to put a mark on your drill bit two inches from the end, then stop the hole at that point. Use screws a little longer and wider than the drill bit, and hence the hole, so they will have some "bite" into the wood.

Now, go ahead and hang those book shelves!

USING THE SLAP-DASH HANGING METHOD

There are times in life when it's simpler to cheat a little. And I'm a firm believer in doing things the easy way if it gets the job done and doesn't really matter in the long run. So, maybe you don't want to take the trouble to install toggle bolts and no one is going to see the wall behind that shelf after you get it loaded down with your scrapbooks anyway. Okay...

First, find a couple of studs in the area you plan to put the shelf. Put a big X on the wall at those two points. Then take a couple of pieces of scrap wood and nail them to the wall using good long sturdy nails right over the X's, making sure the nails bite into the wood. Slap on a little paint to match the wall and attach your shelf brackets to the scrap wood. It'll work just fine and no one will be the wiser.

PATCHING PLASTER WALLS

Fine hairline cracks in the plaster will give those blah walls some pattern, true, but it isn't necessary to really *patch* hairline cracks. Ordinary chalk will camouflage the damage nicely until you're ready to paint again. Variety and stationery stores carry boxes of chalk in mixed colors and you can probably find one there the color of your walls. Just rub the stick back and forth across the crack until it's filled. Then, take the rest of the box and go play hopscotch with the kids!

A little more effort is required to patch a real crack or hole. First, scrape away some plaster from both sides of the crack with a beer can opener. This is important and necessary to allow the patch a good bonding surface. Don't attempt to mix up a batch of plaster as the professionals do. Just go to the paint store and ask for a can of Spackle. This is a thick, putty-like substance that is ready to use as it comes from the can. Spread a layer of Spackle about a half-inch thick into the crack or hole and let it harden. Repeat with another layer, and as many as are necessary to bring the patch to a level just slightly above the surface of the wall to allow for shrinkage. When the final coat has stiffened but is not completely hard, dip your putty knife or spatula in water and glide it across the patch. This will give you a smooth finish that probably won't need sanding.

Chances are, most of those cracks and holes were caused by someone driving nails into the plaster to hang a picture of Uncle Louie in his graduation suit. It can be done without cracking the plaster but it must be done right. You can avoid future cracks simply by putting two or three strips of cellophane tape on the wall before you drive the nail in. Then, use as small a nail as will hold the picture—and drive *very carefully*.

FIXING BROKEN MORTAR AROUND BATHROOM TILES

No woman can stand the sight of broken or crumbling mortar (that white cement-like substance) around bathroom tiles. It's not only unsightly, but highly unsanitary. You can fix it youself, though, and save a few dollars over calling the tile man (who just *might*, if you're very lucky, show up a week from next Thursday, if it doesn't rain, *and* if he and his brother-in-law don't decide to go deep-sea fishing at Mazatlan off last week's profits).

Ask at the hardware store for *tile grout*, a dry powder that you'll mix with water to a fairly stiff paste (no harder than stirring water into a Betty Crocker cake mix). You'll need about one pound for every 20 square feet of 4 1/2 inch tile, one pound for every three square feet of mosaic tile.

Back home, scrape away the old crumbling mortar to a depth of at least an eighth of an inch. Your pecan pick is a good tool for this job if the tiles are close together. If they're fairly far apart, use a beer can opener.

Mix the grout according to the directions on the bag and press it into the joints between the tiles with a knife. Immediately, go back and smooth the grout and wipe away any excess that wandered onto the tiles themselves. Just wrap a damp rag around your finger for this.

Let it dry thoroughly before you run the shower on it.

FIXING NAILS THAT PUSH THROUGH SHEETROCK

It's quite a shock to look up at the lovely painted walls of your new home and discover that —horrors!—something is suddenly beginning to protrude through the paint at regular intervals up and down the wall. This is a disease of homes one or two years old. Unfortunately, many builders today use lumber which is not thoroughly kiln-dried, or they let the framing lumber sit outside in the rain and become saturated before it's used in the house. It's put up damp and, as you know, wood swells when it's damp. Later, usually just after the builder's guarantee has expired, the wood begins to dry. As it dries, it shrinks, forcing out the nails. That's what you're seeing up there—the nails used to fasten Sheetrock to the framing studs.

I hope you still have some paint left over from the construction of your home. Repairing the damage is simple. The hard part is going to be matching the paint.

With your hammer's claws, remove the protruding nails completely, picking out any bits of cement around them that seem to be loose. Using new nails of the same size, or 4 pennyweight threaded nails, hammer in a new nail a couple of inches below the spot you removed the old ones from. The threaded nails are actually best if you have them because they tend to grip the wood better, as a screw does.

Drive the nails in until they're flush with the wall surface, then give them a good whack so they're slightly *below* the surface of the wall. It may pain you to make this indentation in your beautiful wall, but it's actually necessary for a flawless end product.

Get a bit of ready-mixed drywall cement (or Spackle) from your lumber dealer (you only need a small amount) and fill the holes you made and those left by the original nails. Lather on more cement than is necessary, using your kitchen spatula as a tool, then go back and draw the spatula over the patch. This will level it out. Let it dry, then sandpaper it smooth. If you accidentaly left a low spot, fill it in with more cement and repeat the process.

Brush a little white shellac over the patch and let it dry. Then, paint to match the rest of the wall.

FIXING HOLES IN A SHEETROCK WALL

Nobody's perfect. And, it's no reason to cry just because you rammed your foot through the Sheetrock while practicing for the annual Charleston contest and Volunteer Fireman's Benefit at the Elks Club. You can repair it.

You'll need a piece of Sheetrock (also known as *gypsum board* or *drywall*) that is a little larger than the hole. These come in big 4' × 8' pieces (and I *hope* the hole isn't that big!), so the thing to do is scrounge a piece. Try any home under construction, a neighbor who has done some remodeling lately, or the local lumberyard. If the hole is approximately 3" × 3", get a piece about 6" × 6"; if it's 1" × 2", try for 3" × 4", etc. Cut your scrap into a square or rectangle that will cover the hole with a couple of inches to spare all around. Now, working from the back of the scrap, mark another square or rectangle on the back about two inches in from the outside edge. With your knife, carefully cut into this smaller rectangle, cutting through the paper backing and the gypusm filling. Do *not* cut the paper on the front of the scrap. Remove the outer "frame." You'll end up with a piece of Sheetrock with a paper flange all around it. Carpenters call this plug a *blow-out* patch. Now, place this plug up against the damaged spot and use the plug as a guide to mark on the wall around the hole with a pencil. This is your cutting line on the wall. When you get it cut, you should have a hole that matches the plug fairly closely.

Spread a thin layer of ready-mixed drywall cement all around the opening you've cut into the wall. Put some on the inside edges of the cut, too.

Place your blow-out patch into the hole. Using your kitchen spatula, press the paper flange smoothly onto the cement. Press any excess cement out with the spatula. Now, ladle on a little more cement around the edges of the paper to help blend it into the wall surface. Let dry and sandpaper before repainting.

And practice your Charleston outside from now on!

6

Wallpaper and Wallcovering

Or Whatever You Call It

I have a friend who writes advertising for a "wallcovering" firm. When I asked him, with my usual naivete, what the difference was between wallpaper and wallcovering, he winced and explained to me in measured tones that we do not *use* wallpaper any more on our walls. We use *wallcoverings*. So, this chapter will tell you how to put up that pretty stuff mother called—shhhhhhhhh—wallpaper, which *you* will call wallcovering when you buy it at the store.

Wallcovering is not difficult to apply. If you can cut out a skirt pattern or line the kitchen shelves with shelf paper (shelf covering?), you can paper a wall.

If this is your first venture into wallcovering, I'd advise using one of the pre-pasted papers. There are dozens of pretty ones on the market and they really are easier for the amateur to apply than are conventional papers. However, we'll discuss both types.

MEASURING YOUR NEEDS

The first thing you need to know is how *much* paper to buy. It's very discouraging to get to the store, find a pattern that is so "you" it literally screams "Take me home!" and then go absolutely blank when the salesman asks how many rolls you'll need. You'll either buy too much, wasting the money you really need for a hot-oil treatment, or not enough, or run out halfway around the room. If you go home to measure the room you'll likely find that the pattern has gone out of stock while you were en route.

So, measure first. Measure the dimensions of the room (the number of feet along each wall), then multiply that figure by the height of the wall. For instance, if your room is 12 feet wide, 18 feet long, and 8 feet high, you'll figure 12 feet plus 12 feet plus 18 feet plus 18 feet equals 60 feet, multiplied by 8 feet equals a total of 480 square feet of wall space.

Now, each single roll of wallpaper (oh, the heck with it—it's still wallpaper to me) will cover 36 square feet of wall space. You don't figure it at 36, however. You figure on *30* square feet of paper per roll. This gives you a margin of safety of six square feet for trimming, matching patterns, and waste.

So, 480 square feet of wall space divided by 30 square feet per single roll equals 16. You'll need 16 single rolls to do that room. You *can* deduct one roll for each two doors or two large windows in the room. Don't figure too closely, though. You might make a mistake in cutting one strip and end up short.

We've been using the term "single roll." That is the way paper is figured and priced, but it is actually sold in double and triple length rolls. The reason for this is to give you longer, more usable pieces of paper. Otherwise, you'd have a few feet of short, wasted strips left over from each roll. You know how much more usable Christmas wrapping paper is if you get it on a roll that's twelve feet long rather than in a package of six two-foot long pieces. With wallpaper it's the same difference.

So, if your paper is priced at $1.98 a single roll, you'll actually buy double rolls for $3.96 or triple rolls for $5.94 (or roughly that). To paper our hypothetical room you would need to buy eight double rolls or six triple rolls.

Now, about pattern. Please, for me, resist those flamboyant beauties with three-foot high sunflowers or huge rose-covered trellises, at least for the first time you paper a wall. These patterns require skillful matching at the edges of the paper in order to have a professional-looking repeat of the pattern. If you goof you're going to spend the next year staring at those disjointed flowers and hating yourself for even trying.

Stick to the simpler, all-over patterns the first time. Then, after you've gained a little experience and confidence, paper the whole *world* with sunflowers!

A little advance preparation pays off in successful wallpapering. You'll need to get those walls in good condition before you start the fun part: putting up the paper.

PREPARING THE WALL

Most interior walls today are either plaster or Sheetrock (gypsum board). New plaster, because it contains lime, must be *thoroughly dry* before *anything* is put on it. When it is dry, roll on a flat primer-sealer coat. The wall is then ready for *sizing*. Sizing is a powder you buy at the paint and paper store. You mix it with water, brush or roll it onto the walls, and let it dry overnight.

Previously decorated plaster (either painted or papered) will probably need only the sizing. Before you size, though, remove any loose patches of paper and *feather* out the edges with sandpaper. If there are any holes, fill them with Spackle, let them dry, and sand them smooth. Old paper should be slit in the corners with a razor blade and pasted down. Wipe the walls down with a rag dampened with a strong soap and water solution, and sand any wall painted with a high gloss paint. Then, go ahead and size the wall.

On new Sheetrock with properly taped seams you'll need to roll on that coat of flat primer-sealer, then size the walls.

Previously decorated Sheetrock should be treated much the same as previously decorated plaster. Wash, sand if necessary, patch if necessary, then size.

Do not remove old wallpaper (except vinyls, flocks, foils, and embossed designs) unless it's absolutely necessary. It isn't easy, believe me. You'd have to either steam the paper off with a rented steamer or soak and scrape it off with water and vinegar or a commercial wallpaper remover.

Those elegant vinyls, flocks, foils, and the deeply embossed papers *must* be removed before putting up a new paper, though. Many can be easily peeled off by loosening a corner with a putty knife or spatula, then pulling downward very gently. Wash the walls thoroughly with strong soap, then re-size.

Just as when painting a wall, you'll need to remove the switchplates and outlet plates before you paper. Read the later section on papering over and under outlets—in fact, read this whole chapter!—before actually beginning work.

TOOLS AND TECHNIQUES

You don't need to make a big production of hanging wallpaper, but you *do* need the right tools. A complete kit can be bought at most paint and paper stores for about $5. It'll have a plumb line, seam roller, paste brush, smoothing brush, a razor-blade cutter, along with directions on how to use each. All of these are reusable so the kit is a good buy, I think.

You'll also need a large table. One of those folding aluminum picnic tables is perfect, or you can butt two card tables together.

Remove all switch and outlet plates from the walls.

Never begin papering in a corner, as logical as this may seem. Corners are never straight, so don't let some myopic carpenter's error throw you off. You begin alongside a door. Pick one—any will do. Measure the width of the paper and subtract one inch. Now make a pencil mark on the wall this distance from the edge of that door frame. Take the *plumb line* (simply a weight on the end of a chalked string) and tack it to the wall near the ceiling so the string falls directly across that pencil mark you just made (Fig. 6-1). Hold the weight against the wall and "snap" the string. This will leave a chalk mark on the wall and give you a perfectly vertical line to use as a guide in placing that first strip of paper.

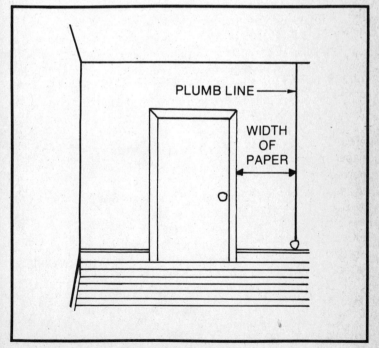

Fig. 6-1. Using a plumb line.

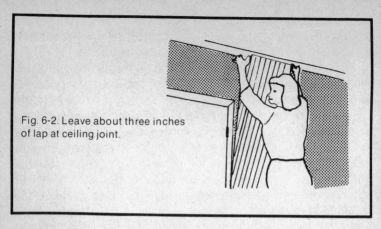

Fig. 6-2. Leave about three inches of lap at ceiling joint.

Cut that first strip of paper six inches longer than the wall is high. This gives you a few inches, top and bottom, for trimming.

Place that strip on the floor or table and, by unrolling another length of paper next to it, cut another strip, matching any pattern at the edges. Be sure you allow that extra three inches at the top and bottom on the second strip. You'll continue to use this matching method for every strip you cut.

If you select a pre-pasted paper, be sure to read the manufacturer's instructions on how long to soak the paper in water before applying to the wall. You'll need a water box for wetting the paper. You can get an inexpensive one from the paper dealer or improvise one from a large roasting pan.

Place the water box on the floor at the end of your table. Roll the cut paper through the water, pattern side down, for the specified length of time. It helps to have some sort of weight to keep the paper in the water as you unroll it. A table knife will do.

Spread the paper on the table, pattern side down, and fold one end over onto itself, paste sides together. Now, fold the other end over, paste sides together. You now have an easy-to-handle package about four feet long.

If you are using unpasted paper follow these directions: Mix the paste in a bucket according to the directions on the box, until it is smooth and completely free of lumps. Let it sit a few minutes, then mix again. It should be about the consistency of very thick cream.

Place the first strip of paper, pattern side down, on the table. Apply paste to one end with the paste brush, using a lazy figure 8 motion. Cover the paper thoroughly and evenly. Fold that end over on itself, paste sides together, and apply paste to the other end. Fold that end over.

From here on, the method is the same, regardless of which type of paper you have. Climb up on your ladder, carrying the folded paper with you. Unfold one end of it and press it lightly onto the wall with your hands, leaving about three inches of *lap* at the ceiling joint and aligning one side with the chalk line (Fig. 6-2). Using the smoothing brush, make even strokes down the paper, adjusting the side of the paper to that chalk line where necessary. Get off the ladder and unfold the lower half of the paper, smoothing and adjusting it as you did for the top half.

You'll find that you have about an inch of paper extra at the sides of the door frame. (Remember, you subtracted an inch from the width of the paper when you drew that chalk line.) This margin should be trimmed off by running the razor blade cutter alongside the door frame. Allow that inch to extend across the wall *above* the door, however (Fig. 6-3).

Take the smoothing brush now and use it to press the paper firmly into the ceiling joint (Fig. 6-4). Trim the paper off neatly at that crease with your razor cutter. Do the same at the baseboard. Some women prefer using a spatula or putty knife to give them a sharp crease at the ceiling joint. They then pull the paper away from the wall a bit and cut it with shears. In any event, smooth the paper on the wall, top and bottom, adding a bit more paste if you feel it is necessary.

A little housekeeping is in order as you go along. Wipe away any paste that smeared onto the paper or woodwork

Fig. 6-3. Trimming margin at doorway.

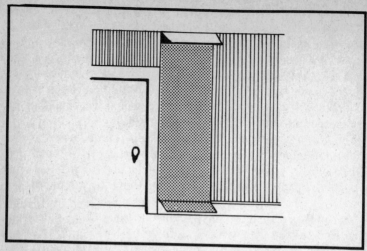

Fig. 6-4. Crease laps at ceiling and baseboard.

before it has a chance to dry. Clear warm water and a sponge will do the trick.

The second strip is hung the same way as the first, using the edge of that first strip as the guiding vertical line. You can make either a *butt* seam by bringing the two edges of the paper together with no overlap. or a *wirelap* seam with just 1/16th of an inch of overlap to guarantee that no wall shows through. The first way is neater, but harder to manage.

Before you know it you'll be near a corner. It may seem logical to hang a strip of paper round the corner and onto the next wall, but don't do it! Remember, that wall isn't straight! You would probably end up with an uncontrollable mass of wrinkles.

Measure the distance from the edge of the last strip to the corner at the top and bottom of the wall, then add about two inches to each of these measurements. Cut a strip of paper that width and hang it as you did the others, allowing that two inches of extra paper to continue around the wall. This little bit can be controlled.

Get out the plumb line again. You need to strike another vertical line as close to the corner as possible on this *new* wall to use as a guideline for the first strip of paper you'll hang on that wall. Make sure your chalk line falls completely on the overlapped strip. Continue as before.

You can hang wallpaper around doors and windows without doing any preliminary cutting if you're careful. Begin

72

hanging the panel just as though the opening was not there, lining it up with the previous strip of paper. Smooth the paper down from the ceiling with your brush until you get near the top of the opening. Then, with your scissors, make a diagonal cut from the *outside* edge of the paper (the edge that extends across the opening) to the top corner of that opening's frame. Smooth the paper into place above and to the sides of the opening and trim with your razor cutter (Fig. 6-5). Do the same at the lower edge of windows.

In your kit will be a small hard rubber roller. Use it to press seams flat and give a professional look to your job. Just roll it up and down each seam, using a firm, steady pressure. Wait at least fifteen minutes after a panel is hung, though, before you roll its seams. And, don't use a roller on flocked paper, ever. It could flatten out that beautiful fluff! Just tap the seams of flocked paper lightly with the smoothing brush.

GETTING BEHIND A RADIATOR

If you have a radiator which is installed a few inches from the wall, you're probably wondering how on earth you'll ever get your hands, the paper, *and* the smoothing brush in there without throwing yourself permanently out of joint.

Easy. Smooth the paper down as far as you can reach with the brush. Then, take a yardstick, wrap it with a bath towel and poke *that* down behind the radiator as your smoothing brush. It works just fine.

PAPERING OVER AND UNDER OUTLETS

You took all those switch and outlet plates off before you even cut that first strip of paper, didn't you? Good. Here are directions on the easy way to paper around those outlets.

Fig. 6-5. Papering around windows.

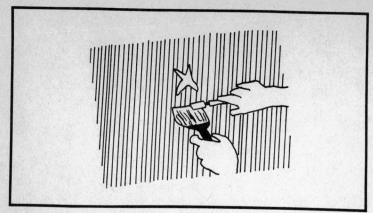

Fig. 6-6. Papering around outlets.

Cover each outlet with a few strips of masking tape. Then paper away, *right over the outlets*. Cover them completely as though they weren't even there. The masking tape will keep the paste from seaping into the holes in the outlets. As you go along, make a small mark on the paper directly over each outlet so you'll be able to find it later. You'll have to poke little holes in the paper for the switches to stick through.

After the paper is dry, make sure the electricity is turned off, go back and cut an opening over each outlet and switch, slightly smaller than the plate which will cover it (Fig. 6-6). Then put the plates back on. (For information on turning off the electricity in that particular room only, see the chapter on electricity.)

For a real decorator touch, paper the *plates* too. You'll have to do a bit of molding with your fingers to get the paper smooth over the slightly curved plate, but the results are absolutely smashing! Don't use regular wallpaper paste. It might not adhere to the plastic plates too well. Use one of the multi-purpose household glues which will stick almost anything to anything. And, of course, paper these plates *before* you put them back up!

GETTING AROUND WALL FIXTURES

Professional paperhangers would take that wall lamp completely off the wall. This involves disconnecting some wires, though, and you may not want to do that. It *can* get a little tricky, and they'll have to be reconnected later. Avoid it by using one of our "Ladies' Specials."

Cut the strip of paper in the normal way. Then, measure carefully the distance the wall fixture lies from the floor up, the ceiling down, and from the edge of the last strip of paper. Measure that same distance on the paper which is to go behind the fixture and cut a large X at the point with a razor blade. What you're doing is making a door for the fixture to slip through. The X must be large enough to allow the fixture to pass through without tearing.

Position the paper in place, peeling back the flaps of that X so the fixture will stick through.

All wall fixtures have a screw which can be removed to allow the fixture to hang loosely from the wall. Turn off the electricity to the circuit serving that room, then remove that screw. Gently slip the fixture through the cut making sure you don't pull those wires apart! Allow the fixture to hang for a minute while you smooth and adjust the paper from floor to ceiling, pasting that X back together again on the wall. You'll probably have to trim the points of the X a bit.

Lift the fixture back into position, replace the screw, turn the electricity back on, and treat yourself to a pat on the back! You did a good job!

USING PAPER BORDERS—GOOD GOOF CONCEALERS

Borders are normally used at the ceiling line of rooms where both the ceiling *and* the walls have been papered. But that doesn't mean you can't use them to camouflage the top line of a wall job only—regardless of *what's* on the ceiling. So, if the top edge of your papering effort is a bit less than perfect, cheer up. Just make a fast trip back to the paper store and get a roll of border paper. It's pasted up the same as the walls only you hang it horizontally instead of vertically, just below the joint between the ceiling and wall. After it's in place no one will ever know that upper edge of your wallpaper once looked like the skyline of New York City!   And, if you don't tell, I surely won't!

PUTTING UP MURALS AND SCENICS

Don't be afraid to try a decorating "dream" like a mural just because the results are so fantastic. They aren't a bit harder to put up than regular paper. More expensive, but no harder.

The main point you'll want to ponder is just *where* on the wall you want to center your mural. Murals and scenics usually come printed on pre-cut strips of paper which are much longer than the height of the average room. This is to give you plenty of leeway as to whether those Japanese cherry blossoms should be at eye level, above or below. It's a good idea to keep the size and placement of your furniture in mind as you decide where to place the central design. You don't want to hide all that beauty behind the china cabinet, and by the same token, those lovely branches might look a bit strange soaring five feet above your low-slung furniture.

Use the same application methods described earlier in this chapter—careful preparation of the wall, a perfect vertical line for the first strip, cleaning up the paste as you go. Then, invite everyone you know in for hot spiced wine. And, *do* try to be modest when you accept all those compliments for being such a smart cookie!

THE INEVITABLE—REPAIRS!

Even the *best* wallpapering job, whether yours or a professional's, will occasionally need repair. If the paper itself is still in good condition those repairs will be childishly simple.

Loose Edges

Pull the paper away from the wall as far as you can without tearing it. Brush a coat of white household glue on either the wall or the paper and press it back onto the wall. Sponge off any glue that oozes out onto the paper. You'll probably need to keep running your fingers over the gluded area for a minute or two until the glue is set. Stubborn edges that keep popping away from the wall can be taped down with masking tape until the glue is dry. The masking tape will pull away easily later without making a mark or tearing the paper.

Bubbles

Got a big dry bubble right in the middle of a long strip of paper? Don't worry, you can fix it without taking down the whole panel.

Just make a neat slit right through the center of the bubble with a razor blade. Push white glue into the cavity using whatever will work—a knife blade, an eye-dropper, etc., and press down. Don't forget to sponge off the excess glue.

Holes and Tears

You can even patch wallpaper if you have any scraps left over. Select a piece of paper a few inches larger all around the damaged area and *tear* it to the desired shape. Do not cut with scissors! Cutting would leave a sharp line which might show. Tearing leaves a feathered edge which will blend with the background paper.

Naturally, you thought ahead and tore off a piece where the pattern is identical with the section of pattern around the hole or tear. Brush some white glue onto the back of the patch and work it around on the wall until you have an exact match of the pattern. Press with your fingers for a minute or two, then sponge off the excess glue.

BURLAP WALLCOVERING

Plain old ordinary burlap is fantastic for covering drab walls and giving them real modern zing. You can buy burlap made especially for wallcovering, with paste already on it, just like paper. However, it's much less expensive to use burlap yardage from the fabric shop. Scout around for one of those discount shops which advertises every month or so, "Anniversary Sale! Five Yards For A Dollar!" This will be your best source.

Measure the number of *feet* around the entire room. This figure will be approximately the number of *yards* you need to cover the walls. Don't deduct for windows and doors unless they are unusually large. Anything left over can be used to cover lampshades or make scrapbook covers, picture frame mats, big rustic shoulder bags, etc.

Sometimes burlap sold this way is badly wrinkled. It helps to iron it reasonably flat, but don't try to get it to look like your best damask tablecloth just back from the laundry. 'Tain't necessary.

Prepare and size the walls as described in the paragraphs at the beginning of this chapter. Cut the burlap into lengths about six inches longer than your walls are high. This is to allow for a lap at top and bottom, and shrinkage. Although not absolutely necessary, it helps to have the burlap damp when you put it up; so, if you can, fill the tub with lukewarm water and put two or three panels in at a time. Let them drain over the shower rod for a few minutes before pasting to the wall.

You'll use virtually the same application methods for burlap as described for wallpaper, with two exceptions. Put the paste on the *wall* instead of on the fabric. And make a generous lap at each seam—at least an inch.

If you have trouble getting the burlap to stick on the wall, try *stapling* the edges down with your desk stapler. Any staples that show can be removed later after the burlap is dry.

Don't be dismayed if the burlap doesn't hug the wall like the postage on your letters. One more step will take care of that. Wait until the wall is dry. Now, you're going to go back over it again—and paste it down from the top! This is my own method and undoubtedly would cause no end of brow-slapping and anguish moans from a professional paperhanger, but it works, and gives you the tightest burlap-covered wall you've ever seen. And, that's what we're after, isn't it? Besides, I think this extra coating helps to seal the burlap against dirt and stains, much as a silicone spray does for your furniture. So, get out the wallpaper paste again, but this time mix it very thin—about the consistency of light cream. With your biggest brush, slosh this mixture all over the burlap. Be sure to protect the floor with some sort of drop cloth because this thin paste will drip.

When *this* dries, that burlap *will* be tight on the wall. And, for fifteen dollars or so, and a lot of bending and reaching which is good for the waistline, you'll have one of the smartest wallcoverings of any gal in your crowd. Don't be surprised if people start asking your advice about decorating *their* dreary pad after they see how you transformed your place into something right out of *House Beautiful!*

7

Painting

It Can Hide A Multitude of Sins

A little well-applied paint can cover a world of abuse, poor construction, and just plain age. (You *know* what warpaint does for your face!) There's magic in color. It can lift your spirits, make a cavernous barn of a room nice and cozy, and camouflage some long-gone-architect's mistakes. Just as you use makeup to contour your face, use color wisely and you'll have a more livable home. Today's easy-to-apply paints, in luscious colors, are the quickest and least expensive way to give your home a revitalizing facelift, so set aside a weekend one of these fine days and have at it!

Light colors, of course, can make a small room seem larger—and yellow, besides being the most cheerful of all tints, is the best of all, next to white, for this enlarging purpose. A yellow kitchen almost guarantees happy "good mornings." Dark green is one of the best colors to bring a wall "in" and make it seem shorter, or to camouflage a tangle of exposed pipes, weird angles, and "nothing" architectural features.

Don't be afraid to use color. The day of safe ivory woodwork is gone forever, thank goodness! Select color the way you do your clothes—to flatter you and give a lift to your spirits. I once acquired an old Victorian white elephant which everyone in town considered hopeless. The twelve-foot ceilings made it impossible to heat during our cold, damp winters and I walked around the house wearing wool socks for three months of the year. The acres of floor space were obviously intended for a day when every house came equipped with a bevy of hefty maids. But for 75 years, families had lived and loved in that house, and I adored it. To revive its dormant Victorian charm I painted one little parlor in brilliant, fire-engine red, to the complete horror of some of my conservative friends. But after I'd painted the fireplace a soft antique white, installed a gilt framed mirror *over* that fireplace, and hauled in all the brass andirons, velvet drapes, and "antique" furniture the budget would allow, my friends were green with envy. My "Molly Brown" parlor was the talk of the town! And the background for the whole lovely room was a couple of gallons of bright red paint. If I had tried to be practical and use peach or sea green, it would have been a completely nothing room.

Ready to tackle a whole room? Here's how!

THINGS YOU'LL NEED TO HAVE
AND KNOW TO PAINT A ROOM

Just like the directions on the home-permanent box say, make sure you have everything you need before you start (Fig. 7-1). Here is a list of what you'll need to complete a paint job with the least amount of trouble:

1. Dusting cloths or brushes to dust walls.
2. Wire brush or stiff bristle brush if you have to remove cracked or flaking paint from woodwork.
3. Empty cans (coffee, large juice, etc.) for cleaning brushes.
4. Drop cloths to protect floor and furniture. Use commercial ones, old sheets, or old bedspreads.
5. Sandpaper if you must smooth rough spots on walls or woodwork.
6. Ladder.
7. Masking tape if you're painting windows.
8. Mixing paddle to stir paint.
9. Rags for cleanup.
10. Roller and roller pan.
11. Brushes of proper size for the job.
12. Proper solvent for thinning paint, if necessary, and cleaning brushes. (Turpentine for oil-based paints and water for water-thinned latex paints.)
13. And, of course, enough paint to complete the job.

Fig. 7-1. Some essential painting equipment.

Start with a clean surface. Just dusting most walls and ceiling will be enough preparation. However, if you're painting a kitchen or bathroom or very badly soiled walls, wash down everything with your household cleaner, and rinse. You don't have to worry about drying the walls if you plan to use latex paint—and I highly recommend using it. Latex paint has to be the greatest boon to us do-it-yourselfers since the invention of the paint roller.

You don't want to run out of paint with half a wall left to do (this always happens on Sunday when the paint store is closed), or end with four gallons of custom mixed Luscious Lavender left over. So, measure before you buy. A wall that's eight feet high and twelve feet long has 96 square feet of space to cover. You don't allow for doors and windows unless they are enormous. So, figure up the amount of wall space you plan to paint and then check the side of the paint can to see its approximate coverage. One gallon will usually do the average

12×12 room. A little arithmetic here can save hours of anguish and frustration later. When you go to buy the woodwork enamel, figure about 35 square feet for each window frame and sash and about 50 square feet for each door and frame.

Have the clerk at the paint store shake the paint on his mechanical shaker, but ask him for a *paint stirrer* and give it a few more good licks with the stirrer after you open the can. Stir rapidly, working the pigment up from the bottom of the can—that is, unless you've bought a paint whose label says "Do Not Stir!"

Begin with the ceiling. You can use either a brush or roller, but why work harder than you have to? The roller is easier and faster. Most rollers have a threaded hole in the handle which will take an extension handle. I found out to my delight, once, that the handle on my garage broom fit my roller brush perfectly. Just one of those lucky flukes we're all entitled to occasionally. You'll have to use a ladder to get up and paint the corners with a brush (the roller won't go all the way into the corners) but, after that, by using an extension handle on your roller, you can paint the whole ceiling from the floor (Fig. 7-2). It's much safer and better that way.

Incidentally, don't pour too much paint into the roller tray. It will spill out when you try to load the roller with paint. Loading it about two-thirds full will do. And, close that can of paint—even if you know you'll be opening it again in ten minutes. One of the joys of latex paint is its fast-drying qualities—and it dries out in the can just as fast!

To load the roller with paint, move it back and forth in the tray until the paint is evenly distributed around the roller. Lift the roller. If any paint drips off you've overloaded it. Squeeze a little out by rolling it across the high back part of the pan (above the paint line). Then, move the roller across the ceiling in slow, smooth strokes, working first in one direction, then in another.

You will probably be using a different color on the walls. It's best to use another roller if you have one, and avoid the possibility of mixing the colors. If, like most of us, though, you only own one roller, wash it out thoroughly in soapy warm water, rinse, and let it drain partially dry before you go on. This is a good time to have lunch, make a few phone calls, or what-have-you. You could also use the time to paint a border

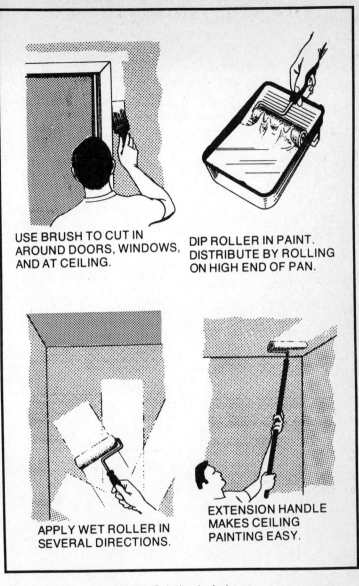

USE BRUSH TO CUT IN AROUND DOORS, WINDOWS, AND AT CEILING.

DIP ROLLER IN PAINT. DISTRIBUTE BY ROLLING ON HIGH END OF PAN.

APPLY WET ROLLER IN SEVERAL DIRECTIONS.

EXTENSION HANDLE MAKES CEILING PAINTING EASY.

Fig. 7-2. Painting techniques.

around the the doors, windows, and upper edges of the wall next to the ceiling with your brush. Make a border four or five inches wide with the brush and there won't be any chance of your roller accidentally bumping the woodwork or ceiling. (Well, *hardly* any chance. We all goof occasionally and leave a swipe of Actually Avocado wall paint on a pristine white ceiling. Don't worry. You can touch it up later and no one will be the wiser. Because latex doesn't leave lap marks, you can go ahead and outline doors and windows in the entire room before starting to work with the roller. It saves much time that way.

Painting the walls is virtually the same as painting the ceiling—use long, smooth strokes up and down, back and forth. It's just a whale of a lot easier on the arm muscles. And, it goes so fast! You can easily do a whole room in one day and still knock off in time for a bubble bath and manicure before the love of your life arrives to take his darling out to dinner!

Just be sure to put on a good coat of paint. It's poor economy to skimp by spreading the paint too thin. Last year's color may shine through and you'll end up having to do the whole wall over.

Wait for the walls to dry (probably two or three hours) before painting the woodwork.

Even though the latex *enamel* you use on woodwork is similar to the latex *flat* paint you used on the walls, you'll notice a slight difference in feel as you flow the enamel on. You should use a brush for enamel. Working on a small area at a time, brush on the paint with horizontal strokes that level off with even vertical strokes. Work quickly and don't go back to touch up a spot that has begun to "set."

Painting windows calls for patience and a steady hand. To make it a little easier, place painter's masking tape along the edges of the glass panes. This protects the glass from accidental smears and when it's pulled off later, you have a nice, sharp edge. Many modern window sashes can be lifted out of the frame entirely for painting (and cleaning). If you have this type, you're in luck. Just take them out to the garage or what-have-you and paint them there. If yours are the kind that seem to be permanently fixed into the frame, adjust the upper and lower sashes so both are clear of the top and bottom of the frame—that is, have them more or less behind one another in the middle of the frame. Paint one, then by adjusting it first up and then down, paint the other. If it's necessary to paint the recessed part of the frame, (the track the window slides in), raise both sashes to the top, and paint the lower section. Wait until the paint is thoroughly dry, lower the sashes, and paint the upper section. This way you avoid gluing the window shut with paint. Then do the frame and sill.

Before you start to paint a door, try to get everyone—dogs, kids, neighbor's kids, etc., either asleep or safely locked outside. It's one of those inscrutable rules of nature that just as soon as you start to paint a door, everyone on one side of it will suddenly need to get to the other side and vice versa. I've threatened more than one dog with sudden extinction for decorating my freshly enameled door frame with tail hair as he dashed out to his daily appointed task—chasing the mailman.

Paint the door frame first. Then do the top, back, and front edges of the door itself. If the door has panels, paint them and their moldings, starting at the top. Paint the rest of the door, then, starting at the top.

The baseboard, which is the piece of wood next to the floor, is painted last. In order to keep paint off the floor or carpet, you should use a protective guide. A piece of stiff cardboard will do. Just hold one edge of it at the very bottom of the baseboard, protecting the floor as you brush the paint onto the baseboard (Fig. 7-3). It doesn't matter if you get paint on the cardboard. Move the protective guide along with you as you go.

If you used the latex paint I suggested, you can clean up everything with warm soapy water. But, do it quickly. Even though they're water soluble, latex paints are on to stay once they dry. If you used an oil-based paint, use the solvent recommended on the paint can for cleanup.

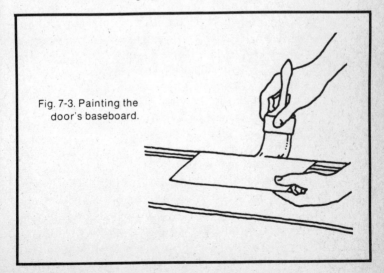

Fig. 7-3. Painting the door's baseboard.

One word of caution before you strike out to become the neighborhood Michaelangelo: almost all household paints are generally harmless, used with adequate ventilation, and washed off the skin immediately after use. But if you find yourself getting dizzy or nauseous, stop immediately! You may be one of the very few who's allergic to paint vapors.

Water-thinned paints are not inflammable. Solvent-thinned paints, varnishes, lacquers, and stains *are* inflammable. *DO NOT SMOKE WHILE USING THEM.* And, resist the urge to have that cozy fireplace flickering away while you're painting the woodwork around it. You can have a fire where you least intended it!

Dispose of all cleanup rags outside if possible. If you can't do that, store them, *loosely,* in a well-ventilated area away from a furnace or radiator until the trash man comes. Turpentine soaked rags can ignite spontaneously and burn the house down if wadded up and thrown into a warm, poorly ventilated closet or storeroom.

Also, keep *all* paint and paint products away from the inquisitive reach of little children. Many of these products can cause serious internal injury if swallowed.

Buying Brushes

Brushes come in a bewildering array of sizes, each for a specific purpose. And, they're not cheap. So, plan to take care of the ones you buy by cleaning them thoroughly and promptly after use. You can get years of service from a good brush if it's taken care of. If you've been painting with water-thinned paint, wash that brush out in soapy warm water and rinse. If you've used a solvent-thinned paint, clean it in turpentine or mineral spirits, using several rinses in solvent. Hang it to dry. Most brushes have a small hole in the handle for this purpose. Then, wrap the brush carefully in plastic wrap or foil to preserve the shape of the bristles, and store until the bug hits you again to change the color of something.

The right size brush is important. You'll need a small two-inch *sash* brush for windows and most molding. A three-inch brush is good for doors and furniture. Then, there are the giant four-inch and five-inch brushes for floors and walls. The price tags will read from $1.50 to $5 depending upon the quality and size. Again, this is no place for false economy. A 79¢ brush is worth about $79 in headaches—and nothing in performance—so don't buy one. Get the one that's somewhere near the middle of the price range. Buy one with bristles that are reasonably long, thick, and flexible. They'll hold the paint better and glide more smoothly over any surface.

Restoring Hardened Brushes

I know I told you to clean your brushes right after use. But nobody's perfect, especially me. And I've brought many a brick-hard brush back to life after I left it "for just a little while" to go do something more interesting, then forgot all about the thing.

Your paint store carries a powder which you mix with water for this purpose. A box of the powder will cost about fifty cents. Mix half the contents of the box with water in an empty half-gallon milk carton, and let your brushes soak a day or two. Wash in strong detergent, then rinse and dry. They'll be as good as new.

SAVING LEFTOVER PAINT FOR FUTURE USE

Leftovers...they're always with us! But, in the case of paint, bless your stars you have every drop because if you actually *live* in that room you just painted, one of these days the wall will get nicked or dirty, and you'll have to patch it.

You *can* leave the paint in its original can. The only problem is that air often creeps in through the lid and you find a thick, rubbery skin on top of the paint when you go to use it again. Actually, this doesn't hurt the paint, it's just wasteful and messy to remove. To help prevent this skin from forming, cut a disc of waxed paper (as you do when lining a cake pan) just slightly larger than the can and lay it gently on the surface of the paint, pressing the edges against the wall of the can. I find it's a good idea to cut this disc before you start painting because when I get through with a paint job of any size, I can hardly wait to get the mess cleaned up and find a place to flop with a cup of coffee. I'm not about to clean my hands, measure and cut the waxed paper, then get all icky again putting it in the can. Put the lid on the can, cover it with a rag or newspaper to discourage splattering, and tap it down firmly with your hammer (Fig. 7-4). If, despite all your precaution, there is a skin on the paint next time you go to use it, don't worry, there's no real harm done. Just cut it away, stir the paint thoroughly and strain, if necessary, through a piece of screen or an old nylon stocking.

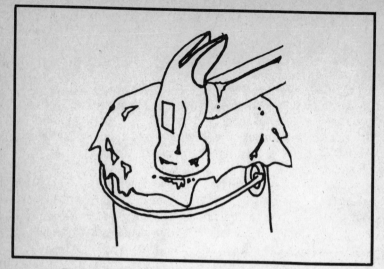

Fig. 7-4. Covering paint can to prevent skin formation.

An even better and tidier way to store leftover paint is to pour it immediately into clean screw-top jars. Tighten the lid the best you can, then label the jar according to which room its contents are from. It's much easier to read "Misty Morning Mauve—front bedroom walls" from a nice clean label than to try to figure out from the drips on the side of a can whether it's the enamel you used in the bathroom or the flat paint from the entrance hall.

I heard of one brainchild who saves her empty fingernail polish bottles, cleans them, and fills them with leftover paint. She does this in addition to the jar bit. The beauty of this is the little built-in brush which is perfect for touching up tiny scratches or camouflaging a nail hole. No searching for a brush, no cleanup, just instant repair. Wish I'd thought of that one!

PROTECT PAINT FROM FREEZING

All paint products should be protected from freezing. This little precaution was taught to me in one fast lesson the first winter I lived in the Rocky Mountains. I had always lived in warm climates before and was accustomed to storing paint in the garage. I painted a room or two, then stashed the leftover paint in my outdoor tool shed (unheated, or course). The coldest night that winter was a mere 30° below zero but did I worry about all that expensive paint stacked neatly away with the gardening tools? Of course not! I got the shock of my life when I opened one of those cans the next spring. The contents looked more like moldy Mississippi River mud than the Deluxe Chocolate Brown Interior latex accent paint I had put away.

At the other extreme, don't store paint in a utility room or closet that also houses a furnace, water heater, or other fire-producing gadget. Summertime temperatures here could conceivably ignite the vapor from solvent-thinned paint.

REPAINTING SECTIONS OF DAMAGED OR DIRTY WALLS

Often one section of a room (around doorways, along staircases, etc.) will become dirty or scarred long before the rest of the walls need repainting, and there's no need to do the whole room if you can help it.

First, wash the area with good strong household cleaner to see if this will help. It's amazing sometimes how much just plain grime we can deposit on our walls. If there's a good coat of paint underneath, you can often just wash away the months of use or abuse.

However, if the paint is scratched or worn off, you'll have to renew it. Don't despair, though. There's an easy way to avoid a complete room renovation by just using your head. This hint only works, however, if you still have some paint left over from the last time the wall was painted. (Another reason to save every drop.) Buying *new* paint, even if the color name and number is the same, doesn't always work because dye lots change from time to time and you can't be guaranteed that the paint will match exactly.

What you're going to do is paint an *area*, not a patch. Patches are obvious. The new coat won't be noticeable, though, if you use the wall's architectural features to help disguise it.

Say the offending area is around the switch plate near a door. In your mind, draw an imaginary line from the top of the door to the ceiling. Begin painting there and paint to the next architectural feature—window, corner, closet, or what-have-you. Stop at the point, again carrying the paint up an imaginary line to the ceiling and down to the floor. Feather it out (that is, use your brush or roller to blend the new paint with the old) along the imaginary line. Our eyes are trained to accept these breaks in the wall and no one will notice your camouflage if you use the breaks as quittin' places. Drapes and furniture will also help.

MATCHING PAINT WHEN
YOU DON'T HAVE ANY LEFTOVERS

Every once in a while you'll need to touch up a small nick in the woodwork, a piece of furniture, or an appliance. Even a small can of enamel will cost at least two or three dollars and you may have absolutely no need for the rest of the can. Don't waste your money. Go to the model car counter of your neighborhood hobby shop or dime store and you'll find a rainbow of colored enamels, in tiny bottles about the size of a gift bottle of Chanel No. 5. Unlike the Chanel, you can buy one of these for about a half-dollar, and they have nice screw-tops. Use the bit you need and reseal the bottle in case you ever need it again.

REMOVING HARDENED PAINT FROM CLOTHES

Nobody in his right mind would pick up a paint brush and can of paint in anything but his oldest clothes. But, I have a closet full of blouses and jeans that are beautifully decorated with every color in the rainbow because I thought, "This won't take a minute, and I'll be careful." Famous last words.

I just learned a trick, though, that saved my favorite navy blue sweatshirt from the rag bag, and I'm going to try it on all those other mistakes. I was doing some painting away from home and wore my old painting clothes. Knowing it would be cool coming home, I threw the sweatshirt in the back of the car. Well, there's nothing as consistent in Colorado as changeable weather. By noon the warm, dry June day had turned cold and rainy and I was *freezing*. On went the sweatshirt. It kept me warm all right, but it got splattered with green latex enamel in the process. I figured it was lost and relegated it to the end of the closet.

I *liked* that sweatshirt, though. So, figuring I had nothing to lose, the next day I ran it through the washer, not really expecting the paint to come off. It didn't. My Irish stubbornness took over, then. While the fabric was still wet, I took my kitchen bottle of Pine-Sol and doused each spot with the disinfectant. Why Pine-Sol and not one of the other cleaners under the sink? Very logical. It was the only one I could reach in that dark cavern jammed with Coke bottles to be returned, bird seed, potted plant food, and garbage bags.

I let the pine oil soak in a few minutes then began rubbing the fabric between my fingers. Miraculously, some of the paint flaked off. Overjoyed, I rubbed in more pine oil and attacked the spots with a brush. Within an hour, there wasn't a trace of the paint and my good old sweatshirt was decent again.

You might give it a try.

PAINTING RADIATORS

You know how durable a baked enamel finish is. You can give your radiators much the same hard, protective cover the next time you paint them if you will have the metal moderately warm when you paint. The finish will last much longer than if painted when hot or cold. The warmth tends to bake the paint onto the metal. Just be sure to use an enamel especially intended for radiators. Regular enamel won't work.

PAINTING REDWOOD OR RED CEDAR

Redwood and red cedar are pretty woods just as they come from the lumberyard and, in time, they mellow to a lovely soft tone. They actually don't need painting at all. If for some reason, however, you want to paint furniture or house trim made of redwood or red cedar, you'll have to *prime* the wood first because the wood can contain substances which will *bleed* through, ruining the finish. Priming is simply a first coat, used before the paint, to seal the wood fibers. Use the one recommended on the can of paint, and that one only. Then, go ahead and paint.

REVIVING A REFRIGERATOR

A sick looking refrigerator can ruin the looks of even the coziest little kitchen. If it works all right, resist the urge to call Goodwill for pickup, and just give it a fresh face with some new paint (yellow?).

You'll need to sand it down first with fine sandpaper, then wash and rinse to remove any possible airborne kitchen grease. You could use one of those exceptionally durable (and expensive) epoxy enamels, but they're hard to apply. Good quality high-gloss enamel will do just as well and will be a lot easier to work with. Use two coats, sanding lightly in between, for a really deluxe finish. Then invite a friend in for tea and rum cookies. She'll think you just got a raise!

FIXING SLIPPERY BASEMENT OR PORCH STEPS

Slipping down a flight of smooth-surfaced basement or porch steps can be a bone shattering experience, and expensive, if the one who fell happens to be a damage-suit-conscious guest.

You can avoid this disaster by installing rubber treads on the stairs. Or, you can repaint them, adding fine sand in equal parts to the enamel you use. Paint as usual, stirring the paint frequently to keep the sand suspended. The dried finish will be slightly gritty and practically skidproof.

PAINTING WICKER FURNITURE

There's nothing as cool and inviting on a warm summer day as a front porch full of freshly painted wicker furniture. So this is one of the times it pays to invest in an aerosol can of spray paint. Painting wicker with a brush is a losing proposition. Sand the furniture lightly, then spray away. Add a pitcher of icy lemonade, the sensuous odor of gardenias, a book...ah paradise!

PAINTING WINDOW SCREENS

Most window screens, except plastic and copper, need the protection of regular painting to prevent rusting. Screen paint (and most any quality exterior enamel will do) applied by brush tends to clog up the holes. The best applicator is a piece of low-pile scrap carpet tacked to a block of wood. Pour a small amount of paint into a flat pan (those aluminum pans that come with frozen pies are perfect), dip the carpet block into it and rub across the screen. Paint both sides. It will probably splatter so wear your grubbies. After you're through just toss the pan and block into the garbage.

If you have many screens to paint, are short of time, and want to invest in a couple of cans of aerosol paint, use the domino method. Stack several screens up against a fence or garage (with something behind the screens to protect them) and spray away. After you've done on one side, turn them around and do the other. This is pretty effective but you may find you'll have to go back and touch up a few missed spots.

Copper screening should not be painted. Instead, clean it with soap and water, then coat it with spar varnish, using either of the methods above.

PAINTING OVER SURFACES IN
POOR OR UNPREPARED CONDITION

It doesn't do any good to paint over a mildewed wall. Before long, you'll see that mildew creep right on through the new paint. You must get rid of it first. Go to the paint or hardware store and get a small amount of trisodium phosphate. Mix this in equal portions with chlorine household bleach and detergent—that is, 1/3 trisodium phosphate, 1/3 bleach, and 1/3 detergent. Then, dilute this mixture three to one with warm water (3 parts mix, 1 part of water) and brush it onto the mildewed surface. Protect your hands because this is strong stuff. Wait an hour or so, then rinse the treated area thoroughly with clean water and let dry. Now it's ready for painting.

Flaked and chipped paint should be scraped and sanded smooth. This will probably remove any original primer or re-prime with the type recommended for the paint you're going to use. Prime all cedar and redwood with a special primer-sealer to prevent bleeding of their natural colors through the paint.

All bare wood or metal must be primed before painting. The type of primer depends entirely upon the surface and the type of paint you are using. After you select a paint, read the label carefully to determine what type of primer it requires, and use it. You may balk a little at this extra effort—after all it's that beautiful finish coat that shows—but believe me, it's worth the time and energy to prime a badly worn window sill or galvanized gutter before you let go with the gorgeous colors. Like the girdle you endure under that slinky knit dress, it's what's underneath that makes what's on top look good.

In most cases a very thin coat of paint will do on wood. Metal requires special primers according to the kind of metal. Ask for them at your paint store. Galvanized steel gutters should weather several months before painting if this is possible. Then a galvanized steel primer should be used before painting (Fig. 7-5). Otherwise, your gutters will soon be covered with ugly splotches of peeling paint.

Glossy surfaces in good condition should be sanded lightly to enhance the adhesion of the next coat of paint. Rusting nailheads should be brushed clean with plain steel wool or a steel brush and then treated with a rust-inhibitor.

PAINTING MASONRY

For some reason which makes absolutely no sense at all, we will cheerfully tackle almost any paint job, as long as it's on a wooden base. Why the thought of painting concrete is so

Fig. 7-5. Special paint for galvanized steel.

traumatic I'll never know because there's virtually no difference.

The most important thing to remember when painting masonry (concrete block, stucco, stone, brick, poured concrete, etc.) is the alkalinity factor. All masonry contains alkali at first. It's built into the chemistry of the stuff. With age and weathering, most masonry will become relatively free of alkali unless the masonry comes in contact with dampness. You can paint even masonry that is loaded with alkali if you treat it first.

There's no need for this treatment, though, *if you use the right paint*.

Now let's all hear a cheer for LATEX! Any latex paint designed for use on masonry can be used on *any* masonry, whether it's five days old or five hundred years old, because latex is inherently resistant to alkali. Just be sure you buy latex paint that says on the label "For Masonry." Don't try to use up the half gallon left over from the kitchen cabinets or the basement wall. It won't work, believe me.

There are other masonry paints, but don't bother with them. Latex is easy to apply, inexpensive and the brush and you will clean up with soap and water.

There are two exceptions to the rule on painting masonry. Cinder blocks have high acid and iron content, along with the alkalinity, and should be painted with a solvent-thinned rubber base paint. And, floors, decks, porches, and patios need a regular rubber base floor and deck enamel. Just read the label to make sure you're buying the right kind.

EXTERIOR TRIM, WINDOWS, DOORS, PORCHES, STEPS

I honestly don't recommend your taking on the job of painting the entire exterior of the house. It's a back-breaking task that requires all sorts of special equipment, especially if you have a two-story home.

There's no reason, though, that you can't spruce up the *trim*. Shutters, doors, windows, the porch and the steps are no harder to paint than your bedroom walls and woodwork (Fig. 7-6).

One thing you need to consider is the weather. Wait until you can depend on reasonably warm, dry days. Most paints should not be applied at a temperature below 50 degrees. And don't begin if the weatherman says a storm is brewing.

A little dampness (dew, yesterday's rain, etc.) won't matter if you use latex paint. If using an oil-based paint, wait several days after a rain for the wood to dry out thoroughly, and several hours after sunrise for the morning dew to evaporate.

Painting windows involves a bit of preliminary inspection. Is any of the putty loose? If so, scrape it out and put on a layer of fresh putty (this procedure is described in the section on replacing window glass in the chapter on windows and doors). First paint the wooden members which divide the window panes, then the frame, and finally the trim, sill, and apron.

Shutters are easier to paint if you can take them down from the house and work on a flat surface. Usually, this will involve removing a few screws from the hinges. It's worth the

Fig. 7-6. Painting windows and shutter.

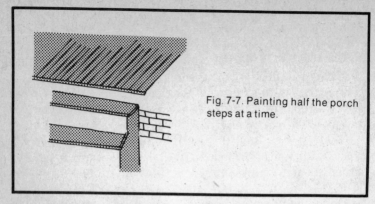

Fig. 7-7. Painting half the porch steps at a time.

little effort in time and arm muscles saved later. Dust and wash the shutters, if they need it, before starting to paint.

Painting an exterior door is no different from painting an interior one. You will, however, have to leave it propped open for a few hours until the paint dries, so do this first thing on a warm day you plan to be home, with the door open all day.

If you're going to be painting the porch *and* the steps, you'll have to put up some sort of barricade to keep people off until it dries. If only the steps are on the weekend list of things to do, you can still paint them and not have your Saturday night date or company get stuck tight halfway to the front door. It takes two days to do it, though. Just paint the *right* side of the steps on Saturday morning and barricade them, leaving the left side open. On Sunday morning, paint the *left* side and barricade it, leaving the right side open for whatever you managed to snag for the afternoon (Fig. 7-7). Neat, huh?

PAINTING INTERIOR STEPS AND STAIRS

You may feel a little like you're playing leap-frog for a couple of days, but the best way to paint interior steps is to do *alternate* steps on one day, the rest on the next day. For instance, on Saturday you paint steps one, three, five, seven, etc., and you walk up on two, four, six, eight, etc. On Sunday, you paint two, four, six, etc,. and walk on one, three, five, etc.

PAINTING PARTICLEBOARD

Particleboard is one of those wonders of the modern lumber industry. You've probably seen it—an ultra-smooth sheet of building material (used on counters, shelving, display boards, doors, tabletops, etc.) which looks as though it's composed of thousands of irregular wood chips, held together with some sort of adhesive. Well, you guessed right! That's exactly what it is—wood particles combined with resins and wax and pressed into very attractive panels which have a million uses.

Particleboard should *always* be covered with some sort of protective covering like paint or varnish. Otherwise, it soils easily and sometimes develops an unpleasant odor.

If possible, find out whether the particleboard you're getting ready to paint is unfilled or was factory-filled, ready for finishing. The unfilled particleboard must have a prime coat of wood filler to seal it. The factory-filled particleboard is ready for painting. If in doubt, use a filler. It won't hurt anything and you'll have better results.

You may use any ordinary paint or varnish on particleboard with good results. However, if you're using a solvent-thinned paint, brush a coating of shellac onto the particleboard first. Particleboard contains a small amount of paraffin wax added during manufacture to retard water absorption. This wax may be dissolved by the solvents in certain paints, causing unnecessarily slow drying. The shellac will form a thin barrier coat to protect the board from the solvents in the paint.

Latex (water-thinned) may be used on particleboard, but it's a good idea to apply a primer of enamel undercoater or white primer first. Particleboard is more porous than ordinary wood and water-based paint tends to roughen its grain slightly unless protected with an undercoat.

Light stains and varnish are lovely on particleboard. Both tend to play up its interesting pattern. Just follow the directions on the can for application.

PAINTING HARDBOARD

Hardboard is a smooth building material, often a dark brown before painting, made by reducing natural wood to fibers and then pressing the fibers together into panels of various thicknesses and surface dimensions. Heat and pressure applied at the factory give hardboard an especially dense character.

Painting hardboard is no different from painting any other raw wood. You first prime, then put on the decorative top coat. Occasionally, you may be using a hardboard which has been factory-primed, but be sure of this before you try to skip the first coat. If in doubt, prime.

First countersink (which is a carpenter's term for using a nail set to drive nailheads below the surface of the material) all nailheads and cover the indentations caused by the countersinking with putty, Spackle, or plastic wood. Sand smooth and proceed with the priming. Use whatever is recommended for the type paint you're using.

SIMULATING STUCCO WITH PAINT

Want to get a rich stucco effect on those plain walls and ceilings? You can transfer that lowly pad of yours into a veritable Spanish palace (well, almost) in one fell swoop by using sand paint. This is a thick paint which dries with a heavy stone-like texture. The trick is in the application.

For a low relief effect, you can put on a thick coat of sand paint with your brush—only instead of brushing in nice, orderly lines, you swish and swirl your brush across the surface as you go, creating a lovely pattern.

For a really dramatic high relief effect, though, forget the brush and use a whiskbroom! Just dip it into the paint and swirl away. Use short, curved strokes of varied lengths and directions. You'll get a very realistic stucco effect.

The beauty of sand paint is that it will cover almost *any* minor imperfection on your walls and ceilings—small cracks, poorly installed Sheetrock, nail holes, etc. And it is one of the hardest interior paints you can use.

So, go on—paint yourself a Mediterranean villa. Ole!

BLEACHING LIGHT-COLORED WOODWORK

The very light-colored woodwork used in so many new homes a few years ago is pretty—when it's light-colored. Unfortunately, it often darkens with age. If you'd like to restore yours to its original finish you'll need to determine first what was put on *over* the wood as a protective finish. Wax alone can be removed with turpentine. Varnish must be stripped off with a commercial paint remover. (Directions for removing paint and varnish appeared in the chapter on furniture.)

After you're down to the bare wood you can bleach it. Paint and hardware stores carry a commercial pre-mixed bleaching compound. Ordinary laundry bleach will work, too, or you chemists in the class can make your own solutions by dissolving a half-pound of oxalic-acid crystals (also from the paint store) in a half-gallon of water.

Brush on this solution very generously and let it dry. As it dries you'll notice a white powder beginning to appear on the wood. Wipe this off with a clean rag. If the wood is as light as you'd like, wipe it down with denatured alcohol and finish off with varnish or lacquer. If it's still darker than you want, repeat the bleaching process until you're satisfied.

STAINING

Wood is a beautiful product of nature, and there are times when it's a shame to cover the lovely grain and color with paint. If you feel this way about something in your home, you want to stain it, not paint it.

The grain of wood cannot be changed. However, the *color* of raw wood can be changed, and often is, to enhance that grain. Stains are available in a wide variety of natural wood tones—maple, walnut, birch, mahogany, etc.—so you can actually take a pale pine wood, for instance, and transform it into expensive "maple" with very little effort! This is often done with paneling. You'll also find exciting colored stains in your paint store, stains which actually dye the wood blue, green or what-have-you, while allowing the grain to remain prominent. The creative possibilities with colored stains are fascinating. Just imagine your conservative middle class home with a smashing turkey red door! Why, you'd be the talk of the neighborhood! However, stain must be applied to bare wood, so don't try this if your door has a layer of paint on it. You must remove that old paint first.

There are several types of stains on the market, but the one you want to ask for is oil stain. It's the easiest for the amateur to use, and practically foolproof. *Never* use varnish stain on anything that is going to show. It may seem like a time-saver to have the varnish and stain in one vehicle, but the results are what you've seen on cheap furniture—a high gloss with all the color right on the surface, not in the wood.

Since a stain merely *highlights* wood, and does not hide very much, it is important to prepare the surface well. Raw wood usually requires only a thorough sanding. Sand *with* the grain of the wood, never across it, with fine sandpaper until it is satiny smooth. Then, dust.

Wood which has been previously painted, such as your front door, must have the paint removed with a commercial paint and varnish remover. This is available in your paint store. It's potent stuff, but not hard to use. The directions for each type (some wash off with solvent, some with water) are on the can. Follow them. Then, proceed with the sanding because you're now down to bare wood.

It's a good idea to test your stain first on a piece of scrap wood, or a spot that won't show, to determine how porous the wood is. Some wood is very porous and will absorb the stain too readily, causing it to take a darker color than you might want. In this case, apply a coat of wood sealer. This will give you a good base for the stain.

Stir, stir, stir is the watchword when you're staining. The pigments in stain settle quickly and it's necessary to stir often while you're working or you'll have one section of your work darker than the other. The can will probably say to use either cloth or a brush to apply the stain. I prefer a brush. It's less messy and seems to do a better job.

Brush the stain *with* the grain of the wood, working on only a small section at a time (one panel of a door, one cabinet door, etc.), then immediately go back and wipe off the excess with a wadded rag. The longer stain stays on wood, the darker it becomes. You can always go back and put on another coat if the first is too light, but it's hard to reverse the process. If you should accidently get the wood too dark, quick like a bunny, soak a rag in turpentine or mineral spirits and scrub the wood vigorously. This will lighten it considerably.

You'll need lots of soft rags for the wiping step. Keep turning the rag as it gets soaked with stain, and discard the rag when there's no clean place left on it.

Most stains require some sort of finish coat, usually varnish. But wait at least a day or so before you get on with that. Stain should dry *thoroughly* before the final finish.

You don't *always* have to follow through with varnish, though. I once stained about a million boards for the ceiling of a summer cabin using a method taught to me years ago by a delightful little old lady in an antique shop. I wanted an old, un-shiny finish, but still wanted to protect the wood, and her formula was perfect. You mix equal parts of boiled linseed oil and turpentine, then stir in enough stain to color the wood the shade you want. Begin with just a tiny bit of stain, and experiment on scraps of wood, adding more and more until you get the right shade. The linseed oil acts as a dressing for the wood, and the turpentine thins the oil to a workable consistency. By adding ' the ' stain, you are actually accomplishing two steps in one, protection and color.

MINI-ITEMS TO SAVE TIME
AND TEMPER WHEN PAINTING

Right after you open a can of paint, and before you begin painting, take your hammer and a large nail and hammer several holes into the groove around the top of the can (Fig. 7-8). That way, the paint you wipe from your brush will drain back into the can instead of building up and running down the sides!

If you're working on something that doesn't require moving the can of paint often, rest it on a paper plate. This will catch any drips and give you a place to rest your brush, too.

There is a little gadget available at paint stores which makes painting window sashes a snap. Logically, it's called a sash painter and will cost you less than fifty cents. A square of fabric much like that on the top of self-polishing shoe polish bottles is attached to an angled handle. You dip the fabric end into the paint and draw it along the sash. With just a bit of practice you'll find you can paint those devilish little wooden dividers between window panes with ease—and no paint on the glass!

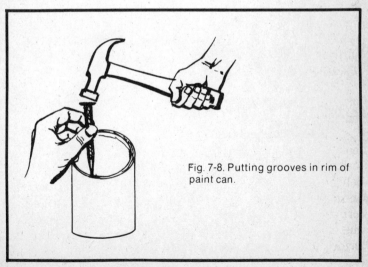

Fig. 7-8. Putting grooves in rim of paint can.

Coat door knobs, telephones, and anything else you're likely to have to touch while painting, with a liberal coating of petroleum jelly before you start. Any fingerprints you leave can then be easily wiped away.

Coat *yourself*, hands, arms, face, and neck liberally with baby oil or cold cream before you begin painting. This keeps strong paints and solvents off your precious skin and makes cleaning up later easier.

To save cleaning your roller tray, line it with a large piece of plastic from a cleaner's bag before pouring in the paint. When finished, just lift it up and throw it in the garbage.

If you're going to continue painting later in the day or the next day, you can avoid two cleanups by wrapping your brushes and rollers tightly in plastic wrap between sessions. Or, submerge them in water if you're using latex paints.

Run out of masking tape and need something to keep paint off windowpanes? Just cut newspaper the exact size of the panes, dampen, and press onto the glass. It'll stick firmly long enough for you to paint the window, then it will peel off easily after it's dry.

Have trouble with the nozzles on your spray paint cans clogging up? They're removable, you know, so just keep a tiny jar of paint thinner handy and drop each nozzle in after you're through painting. The thinner keeps the paint from clogging the tiny holes and you'll find them clean and ready to fit on the can next time you need to touch something up.

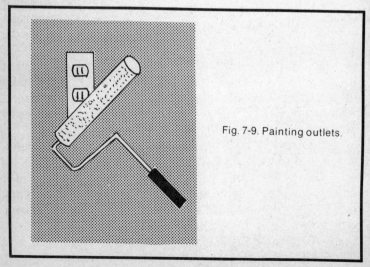

Fig. 7-9. Painting outlets.

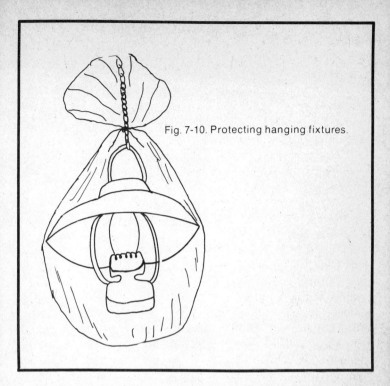
Fig. 7-10. Protecting hanging fixtures.

Nobody wants to have ugly brown outlets ruining the looks of a freshly painted light-colored wall, so paint them, too. But you don't want to clog up the prong holes with paint. An easy way to avoid this is to insert short pieces of frozen sucker or lollipop sticks into the prong holes, then roll your paint right over the receptacle (Fig. 7-9). Later, go back and remove the sticks, using you *fingers*, not tweezers or pliers.

You'll probably want to take your good light bulbs out of the fixtures before you start painting, yet an accidentally dropped blob of paint in an empty socket can ruin the fixture. Think ahead and save a few burned out light bulbs or fuses by filling those sockets.

To protect a hanging light fixture from splattered paint, cover it with a plastic bag from the cleaners (Fig. 7-10).

Paint doesn't keep indefinitely. If, upon removing the lid of an old can of paint, you detect a foul odor, lumps, or curdling, throw the whole thing away. It's spoiled and beyond redemption.

The final work and gospel about painting...if all else fails—read the label!

8

Pipes and Plungers and What To Do With Them

Even on television commercials, lady plumbers do not exactly fit the usual American ideal of wide-eyed femininity. *Not* that you don't have what it takes to be a plumber under that curly mop, but serious plumbing is a dirty job that requires the arms and back of a college football hero. And, many of us don't want to develop those, do we?

There are, however, a few basic and minor plumbing jobs you can handle yourself. Even though you've never attempted anything more complicated than pushing a shampoo attachment onto your bathtub faucet, give these hints a listen. They really aren't difficult. And with plumbers getting ten and fifteen dollars an hour, portal to portal, it'll be worth your time to know how to handle the small emergencies.

The repairs you might try come under four broad categories: repairing water faucets, repairing the toilet mechanism, unclogging drains, and thawing frozen pipes. This chapter will tell you how to do these things, plus it will provide a few other hints I've included in the interests of your solvency.

DRIPPING WATER FAUCETS

A dripping faucet is almost always caused by a worn-out washer. When you *see* this washer you'll wonder how such an insignificant little piece of flotsam—worth maybe ten cents on the open market—could cause so much trouble. To stop the leaking, though, you'll have to replace that washer. This means dismantling the faucet to get to the washer. You'll need a pair of pliers or an adjustable wrench, a screwdriver or two, and the new washer. If the hardware store is within a few minutes' walk and it is a nice day, you may want to take the old washer down there for a match. If the hardware store is, however, three bus transfers and a two-mile-uphill hike away, and only open on Thursdays if it isn't raining, then live dangerously and buy a small box of assorted faucet washers the next time you pass the door. They don't cost much and one of them will fit.

Do you realize that you are about to save yourself at least $10 in plumber's fees for a little repair job that's not much more difficult than replacing a broken sewing machine needle? This has to be the biggest bargain in the whole book.

Now, down to the nitty-gritty. Locate the shut-off valve underneath the sink. It will be prominently attached to the pipe which leads to the dripping faucet. Turn it until it's tight. The water will not flow through that faucet until you turn it on again, so don't do it if your roommate or kids are waiting outside the door to brush her/their teeth. It's going to take you fifteen or twenty minutes to complete the job. When you turn that valve, you've effectively put an "out of order" sign on the lavatory until you're through.

Disassemble the faucet. This involves removing a screw at the top of the handle. On older faucets the screw will be in plain sight. On more modern ones it will probably be hidden beneath a decorative button labeled "H" or "C." Pry the button off and remove the screw (Fig. 8-1).

Lift off the handle. You'll see a brass *valve stem* and *packing nut* which are the heart of the faucet (Fig. 8-2). Don't let those unfamiliar terms throw you. It is a very simple mechanism.

If you have an adjustable wrench, place its jaws around the packing nut, the large six-sided nut at the base of the valve stem, and twist until the whole thing comes loose. Lacking a wrench, wrap some cloth around the nut and use your pliers. The nut may be difficult to remove if it hasn't been taken off for some time. But, give it all you have, and it will turn eventually.

A few turns and the whole brass assembly will lift out in your hand. Turn it over. You're looking at the washer, the

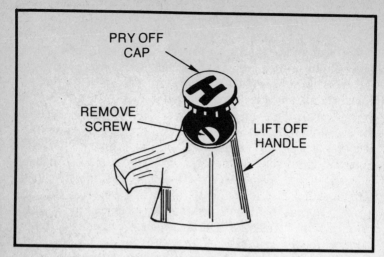

Fig. 8-1. Dismantling a faucet.

troublesome little beastie. It is simply a small round piece of black rubber with a brass screw through its center (Fig. 8-3). Remove the screw and the washer, and replace them with a new set.

While you have the valve stem and packing nut out, wrap a soft cloth around your screwdriver and use this to clean the hole which the assembly fits into (Fig. 8-4). This hole is called the *valve seat* because the whole thing sits in it.

Now, reassemble the faucet by replacing the stem and packing nut and tightening them well. Put the handle back on,

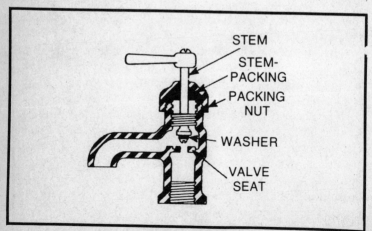

Fig. 8-2. Faucet anatomy.

Fig. 8-3. The troublesome washer.

then the screw, pop on the little button, and turn the water back on.

Now, call in your roommate or kids. She/they can now brush her/their teeth from a faucet that doesn't drip anymore. Aren't you proud of yourself?

TOILET TROUBLES

If you have a toilet that runs continuously or won't flush properly, remove the porcelain top from the tank and examine its interior. You'll see a Rube Goldberg device of float, valves, pipes, and levers which looks terribly complicated (Fig. 8-5). To be honest, it *is* complicated, but a little close examination will show you how the thing works.

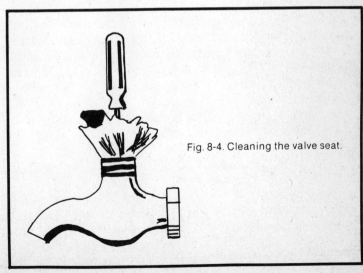

Fig. 8-4. Cleaning the valve seat.

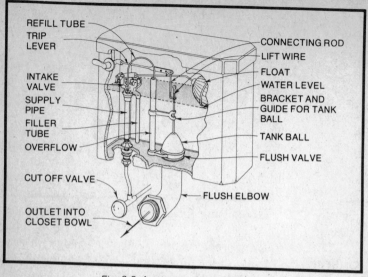

Fig. 8-5. Anatomy of a toilet tank.

Press the handle. You should see it lift a trip lever which is connected to a rod or chain. This part in turn lifts a rubber tank ball off a hole which allows the water in the tank to flow into the bowl, flushing it. Water then flows back into the tank through a pipe, gradually lifting a metal or rubber ball. The water stops flowing once a specified depth has been reached. The depth is determined by the float ball, which trips a shut-off device at that point.

Really, the whole thing must have been conceived by a wild-eyed genius whose mother was frightened by an explosion at a nuts and bolts factory. And if any of you ladies can invent a better method I will personally send you my check for a full year's water bill at your place, because *I'd* like to see a simpler mechanism on the market!

Anyway, if anything disturbs the whole diabolical chain of events, the toilet does not work properly. Let's take the possibilities one at a time.

Toilet That Does Not Flush

If the toilet handle flops up and down in your hand with no tension and does not cause the toilet to flush, check to see if the lever may have fallen off the handle's shaft and be lying at the bottom of the tank. If that's the case, simply fit it back onto the shaft and you'll be in business. Some models have a small set screw which should be tightened once you get the lever back onto the handle.

Toilet That Runs Constantly

A toilet that runs constantly is awfully annoying besides being a terrible waste of water. It's bad for the nerves, the water bill, and the environment. So, if yours is acting up, let's do something about it.

The trouble may be a tangled chain which won't let the tank ball fall fully into place on the outlet. Just work it straight with your fingers. Or, if your mechanism has a metal rod instead of a chain, it may have corroded to the point that smooth operation up and down is hindered. If so, rub the rod vigorously with steel wool until it is shiny and smooth again.

The rubber tank ball may be so old and decrepit that it has gone soft and won't fit snugly onto the outlet, allowing water to seep under its rim. Remove it from the lift rod or chain and take it to the hardware store for a replacement.

To stop water from flowing into the tank while you're out getting the replacement just prop the float ball up with a piece of wood or turn off the valve at the base of the toilet.

The float ball must float at the right level or water will continue to flow into the tank. If it develops a leak, it will become partially filled with water and will not rise high enough. If yours is not floating on a horizontal level you can be pretty sure this is the problem.

A brass float can sometimes be drained and repaired with liquid metal. Good quality plastic may be repaired with waterproof adhesive. A rubber float with a leak must be replaced. To get it out, prop up its rod and unscrew it from that rod. Then, repair or replace it with a new one.

Toilet Flushing Incompletely

Sometimes a toilet will warn us that it is getting ready to go on strike by flushing half-heartedly or incompletely. This is usually a sign that there is some obstruction in the drain.

You'll need toilet auger, or *snake*, to dislodge any clogging mass. The snake is a weird-looking device consisting of a long metal coil with a hook on one end and a handle on the other. As you rotate the handle the hook spins around in the drain, dislodging the obstruction.

To use a snake, you push the coil down into the drain and begin rotating the handle. It rarely takes more than a few minutes to get the drain flowing again.

Fig. 8-6. Removing strainer.

CLOGGED DRAINS

Drains become clogged when something stops waste water from flowing down the pipes. The drainage system in the average home is a masterpiece of efficiency but it was not built to handle hairpins, chicken bones, or that 11″ × 16″ of your ex-boyfriend, the heel. So, an ounce of prevention is worth a pound of plumber's bills later.

You can open most clogged drains yourself—that is, those that become clogged from the *inside* of the house. Sewer lines and exterior drains sometimes become clogged from tree roots growing through cracks in the pipe. You can't do anything about this disaster, so call a professional if it happens at your house. He may suggest digging the pipes up and laying them away from the trees. This is good advice.

Grease and soap scum are usually the culprits in the kitchen sink. If you begin to notice that water is taking longer than usual to drain, try pouring a kettleful or so of boiling water down the sink. This will melt most soluble gunk. If it still runs slowly, let the water in the drain cool and try a commercial drain cleaner. But, follow the manufacturer's directions to the letter. These are extremely caustic chemicals. And, never, never, never use them if you have a garbage disposal.

Bathroom lavatory drains are most often the victims of an amazing amount of hair, glued into a virtually impenetrable mass with soap scum. Now, none of us is going to give up shampooing our locks just to keep a drain clear, for heaven's sake, so it pays to know what to do when the inevitable happens.

First, see if the trouble lies *above* the *trap*. (The trap is the "U" shaped pipe below the sink.) Most modern strainers and stoppers lift out easily for cleaning (Fig. 8-6). If yours is one of these, remove it and see if there's a tangle of icky gunk below it. If so, lift the mess out with tweezers, a crochet hook, or anything else you can find.

The disc-type strainer, a flat piece of chrome with holes in it, has to be removed by loosening a screw in its center. Another, a valve-type stopper which works by lifting and dropping a knob between the faucet, is connected to a rod beneath the lavatory. It has a screw at the intersection of the rod and the lower part of the stopper. You must remove this screw and pull the rod away from the stopper in order to lift the stopper out (Fig. 8-7).

After you get the gummy mess out, pour hot water through to dissolve any soap scum still clinging to the pipes.

If the obstruction isn't visible, you might try a little commercial drain cleaner. Or, better still, see if you can dislodge the trouble with a plunger. This is the homely object known as a *plumber's friend* and no home should be without it. It's merely a heavy rubber cup attached to a long wooden handle (Fig. 8-8) and it will cost you about a dollar.

To use a plunger you must first stop up the overflow outlet with a rag. This helps to build up pressure in the pipes. Run three or four inches of water into the lavatory and put the cup part of the plunger directly over the open drain. Grasp the handle firmly and work it up and down vigorously to create a strong suction (Fig. 8-9). This usually breaks up any clogging mass after a few minutes.

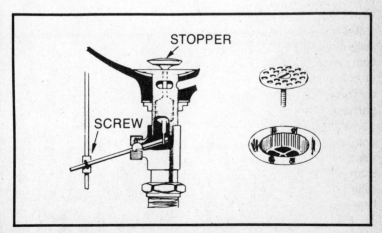

Fig. 8-7. Removing disk- or valve-type strainers.

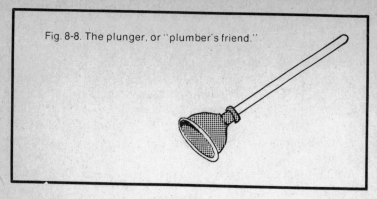

Fig. 8-8. The plunger, or "plumber's friend."

If the drain is still clogged after all this, there may be a solid object, such as a bottle cap, wedged in the trap or drainpipe. You'll need a pipe wrench to remove the trap to find out. Wrenches are pretty expensive and I wouldn't advise buying one just for this emergency as you may never need it again. Ask around the building or neighborhood and see if you can borrow one. With any kind of luck, the man who loans it to you will also offer to come along and do the job. If he doesn't— the unchivalrous clod—it really isn't too hard to do yourself. Put a bucket under the tap. That innocent-looking piece of hardware is full of water and you'll end up with it all over the floor if you aren't careful! Put the jaws of the wrench around the fittings on one side of the trap and twist until they loosen (Fig. 8-10). Repeat for the other side. Gently pull the trap away from the lavatory. Drain the water into the bucket and probe into it with a coat hanger to see if you can dislodge any

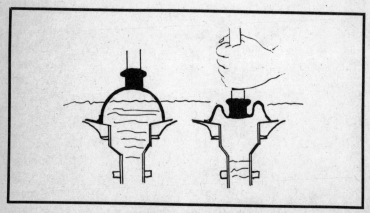

Fig. 8-9. Using the plunger.

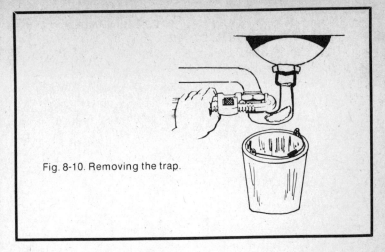

Fig. 8-10. Removing the trap.

obstruction. If none appears, try your toilet auger on the horizontal pipe which leads into the wall. No luck? Give up and call a plumber. The trouble is obviously in the main part of the drainage system and you can't handle that.

But, frankly, I doubt that you will ever have to call the plumber for a clogged drain if you'll follow the first few steps outlined here. Not one time in a thousand will the problem be any farther down than the trap.

If you're a "shampoo in the shower" girl you may have trouble with a clogged tub drain one day. Just follow the same procedures to unclog it as for a lavatory or sink...hot water, a plunger, or a drain cleaner (but *never* a combination of either the first or second with last!). Obviously, since the trap is out of sight somewhere beneath the tub you can't get to it. You probably won't ever need to, though.

A word to the wise. Go to work on the drain as soon as you notice it beginning to flow slowly. Don't wait for a total jam-up. You know that old maxim (remember, I told you I was raised on them!): "A stitch in time saves nine." In this case, the "nine" you'll save will be your temper and the chance for a good hot bath when you want it!

FROZEN PIPES

It's pretty shattering to wake up on a cold January morning and discover you can't get water for your coffee because the pipes are frozen. The really unfortunate part, though, is that dozens of other homes will have the same problem and plumbers will be as independent and inaccessible as a politician the day after election.

Even though you are going to try to thaw that pipe yourself, go immediately to the telephone and call the nearest plumber. He won't be in (some people get up earlier than you and he'll be at their house), but leave word with his wife that you need help. Then, call every other plumber in town with the same sad story. This may sound a little devious but I know families who've waited *days* for a plumber to show up and get their pipes flowing, so it pays to have your name in as many pots as possible.

Now, try to do the job yourself. If you succeed (and it will depend upon how quickly the weather warms up, how hard the freeze was, and where the frozen pipes are located), then all you have to do is call those plumbers and cancel your SOS. And, you've saved yourself a bundle.

If, for some reason, the faucet works but the drain in a lavatory or sink is frozen, you may be able to thaw it from inside the house. First remove the trap according to the directions in the section on clogged drains and pour out the water. Replace the trap. Pour a box of household salt into the drain and wash it down with a kettle of boiling water. If the freezing is not too severe the drain should be flowing in an hour.

More than likely, though, the pipes carrying water into the house will be frozen, too. Check all the faucets in the house to see which, if any, are working. Open the faucts on those that are frozen so the water can begin flowing if you get the pipe thawed.

Put on your warmest clothes now because you're going to have to try to find that frozen pipe. It could be in an unheated basement, alongside the house, or in the crawl space under the house. Work backwards from the faucet to the outside until you locate it. You may be able to actually *see* a small bulge in the pipe at an ice plug. Sometimes you can find the ice by running your hands along the pipe; your fingers will discover the bulge. If you find a plug of ice, begin working at that point. If you can't locate it, simply begin your thawing operations at the end of the pipe nearest the faucet that's frozen and work back.

Never, I repeat, *never,* use a blowtorch or any kind of fire to thaw a pipe. Besides the obvious danger of burning your house down, you could create steam inside the pipe with that extreme heat and cause the thing to explode.

Beginning at the end of the pipe closest to the faucet, try to melt the ice by wrapping rags loosely around the pipe and pouring very hot water onto the rags. The rags help to retain the hot water. Or, if you have a waterproof extension cord, you could hook up an electric heater so the heat is directed toward the pipe. Or, try an electric hair dryer if you have the hand-held type which can be aimed at the pipe.

Just be sure to begin thawing at the end of the pipe closest to the faucet. This way, the water which used to be a plug of ice can run out as it thaws. Never begin working in the center of an ice plug. You could possibly thaw a section there which might turn into steam, and explode. As the plug thaws, move your heat back along the pipe until the water is running freely.

With luck, there won't be any breaks in the pipe. But, if the freezing was extreme, the ice may have expanded to such an extent that it actually split the pipe. A real break will mean a call to the plumber. But you can mend a very small split, at least temporarily, by coating it generously with liquid metal, wrapping with electrician's tape, and clamping as tightly as you can. (There is a hint on making a clamp later in this book.)

If you lucked out and no pipes broke, begin immediately to take steps so they won't freeze again. A temporary solution is to allow the water to trickle from the faucet during a cold snap. Running water doesn't freeze as readily as still water does. Even this practice is no guarantee, though.

You might try insulating the pipes yourself if you live where temperatures do not normally dip too low. There is a fiberglass insulating tape which you can handle. Just begin at one end of the pipe and wrap away. After a foot or so, push the tape together to form a thicker mass and proceed on. You'll have to give it a final wrap of waterproof paper. A cork tape is available in some areas which requires no protective paper covering. In any case be sure you cover all exposed surfaces of the pipe and tie the insulation on securely with string.

The best solution, and the only one for areas which consistently have below-zero readings, is to have the pipes wrapped with electric heating cable. Your plumber can do this. He'll use a special insulated wire which is attached to the house's power supply.

CONDENSATION ON EXPOSED PIPES

You may be "blessed" with a home where beads of water collect on exposed pipes in the basement or bathroom every

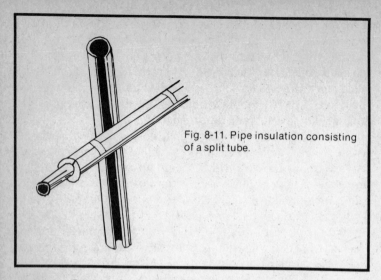

Fig. 8-11. Pipe insulation consisting of a split tube.

summer. It's not leakage, just natural condensation. A mild condensation probably won't cause you any trouble. You should do something about the moisture, though, if it gets to the point that the water is actually *dripping* into puddles on the floor.

All you have to do is wrap those pipes with one of several types of insulation. Your hardware store carries a variety, so check there for the kind you think best for your problem.

One type is simply a tube, sold in three-foot lengths, which has a split down one side (Fig. 8-11). You spread the split open,

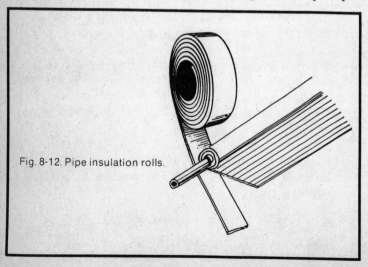

Fig. 8-12. Pipe insulation rolls.

slip it around the dripping pipe, and secure it with a special tape sold along with the tubing.

Another kind comes in rolls—vapor-proof paper on one side and insulating material on the other (Fig. 8-12). Both long edges of the paper have a pressure-sensitive adhesive. You cut a strip of the insulation as long as the pipe. Wrap the pipe, lengthwise, with the paper, and seal with the adhesive edges.

For pipes with bends and curves you might buy a tape made of ground cork and a binder, or a roll of a new self-sticking tape made of foamed plastic. Both are wound around the pipe in a spiral and conform to any shape (Fig. 8-13).

Easiest of all to use is a paint which is mixed with finely ground cork. You just spread it on with a brush (Fig. 8-14).

BROKEN WATER PIPES

What would you do if you came home tomorrow and found water pouring into your living room from a broken pipe in the ceiling? This happens—and I actually saw it twice in the past year, both times in new, luxury homes. Believe me, it is a mess!

The solution is to turn off all water coming into the house immediately. There is a shut-off valve installed in every house, somewhere. It may be in the basement, in the crawl space, on a pipe near the kitchen. *Learn where this shut-off valve is as soon as you move into the house and mark it with a big white tag which can be found in a hurry!* By turning this valve you stop the flood. Then, call the plumber.

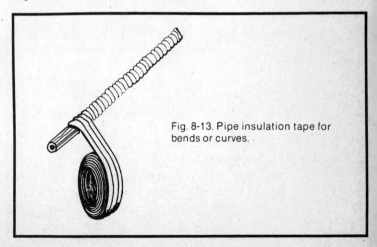

Fig. 8-13. Pipe insulation tape for bends or curves.

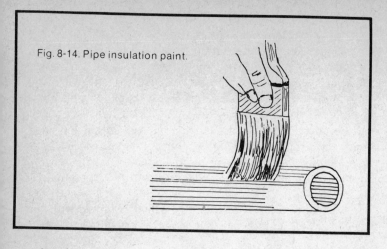

Fig. 8-14. Pipe insulation paint.

Any break *in a fixture* can be controlled by shutting off water to that fixture. Underneath every sink, lavatory, and toilet is a valve which will stop water flowing to the fixture if you just give it a few turns. Take a minute now to look at these valves. I sincerely hope you never have a broken pipe in your home, but just in case...know how to handle it.

WATER HAMMER

Water hammer is a common problem. It is that loud banging and vibration you may have heard in the water pipes. It usually occurs when a faucet is turned off suddenly.

An easy way to stop the problem is to be a little slower when you turn those faucet handles. A more expensive, but also more effective, remedy is to have a plumber install a special shock-absorbing chamber into the plumbing system.

In the meantime, if your house has a tendency toward water hammering, try to find a way to stop the *noise* once it starts. I once rented a house which must have had the worst case of water hammer in the annals of modern plumbing. There were times when I honestly thought the pipes were going to beat their way right through the walls and the whole jerry-built thing would fall down around my ears. Then one day, by accident, I discovered that no matter how vigorously the pipes were vibrating, they stopped *immediately* if I flushed the downstairs toilet! I never figured that one out. So, if you have water hammer at your place, you might try opening and closing different faucets and water outlets the next time it occurs. You just might hit a lucky combination as I did!

9

You and Electricity

It Isn't As Mysterious As It Seems

There *are* lady electricians around, just as there are lady carpenters and lady bricklayers. But, since neither you nor I have had the training to mess around with the wiring in our houses, let's leave it to the experts. This is no place for an amateur.

However, there are a few things you should know about that marvelous electric system that rings doorbells, brews coffee, provides light, and executes a host of other useful tasks in our modern homes.

As you know, the electricity is brought to the house by those big black wires you see hanging outside. At that point, outside, there is a device to either let the electricity *in* to the house, or keep it *out*, at your discretion. This is the *fuse box* or *circuit breaker*. It also serves to turn off the electricity *automatically* if you overload the wiring system with too many toasters, irons, heaters, etc., all burning at the same time.

If one lamp goes out, the chances are that the light bulb is simply burned out. But if a whole roomful of lights and appliances quits at once, you've probably overloaded the circuit. Many older homes don't have adequate wiring to accommodate our wealth of electrical gadgets and when you plug too many in at once, the circuit automatically quits in order to save your house from catching fire caused by burning wires. Even in modern homes, with plenty of heavy wiring for

119

normal use, that ingenious circuit breaker will *trip* if it detects a malfunction in the range or some other appliance that might cause a fire.

Let's take the two types of systems one at a time. Older homes will invariably have a fuse box on the back porch, in the basement, or some other easily reached location. You'll see a series of glass-topped fuses screwed into the box. Each one controls a certain section of the house wiring. When there is trouble in that section of the house, electricity-wise, that particular fuse will blow. The glass will turn dark and the little metal bar which you can see under the glass will break, cutting off current to anything connected to that circuit. You'll have to replace the fuse in order to restore the current.

For safety's sake shut off the house current before you remove the blown fuse.Be sure your hands are dry and you're not standing on wet ground. There's usually a main switch near the fuse box.Or it might be a large lever attached to the side of the box. Or maybe a big switch inside the box itself. In any case, you'll know you've pulled the main switch because everything in the house will go off.

Once the current is off, unscrew the burned-out fuse and replace it *with one of the same amperage*. You can get these at all hardware stores, most grocery stores, most convenience stores, etc. It's a good idea to keep a few on hand so you don't have to go sloshing down to the store at 10:55 on a stormy night to buy one. Worse still, if the thing should blow at 11:15, you'll be out of power in that circuit until morning when something opens up.

Never, never, NEVER temporarily replace a blown fuse with a penny, no matter what some idiot friend may tell you. Sure, the power will come back on because the copper in the penny acts as a conductor of electricity. But that penny can take a tremendous jolt of current—much more than the fuse could take. The fuse is intended as a safety device to blow if something goes wrong. The penny won't blow. So, if there should be real trouble in the circuit, exposed wires, defective range elements, etc., the penny would continue to allow power to flow through the wired—and you *could* end up with a pile of ashes where your home once stood.

Once the new fuse is in, your power will come back on. But, look around to determine, if you can, just *why* it blew. Do you have an electric heater, the iron, a radio, three lamps, a hair dryer, and your saber saw all going at once? In one room? Unplug a few things and move them to another circuit so the same thing won't happen again.

Newer homes with circuit breakers are a little easier to handle. If the power goes off, you just go to the circuit breaker box (it will probably be on the outside of the house), open it, and look for a switch which is turned to the *off* position. This is the switch which controls one particular circuit, and it has tripped because of an overload in that circuit. Simply flip it to the *on* position and you're back to making fondue for your party.

Incidentally, want to know how you can determine just which areas of your house are on which circuit? Plug the vacuum cleaner or an instant-play radio into a wall socket. Open the window so you can hear its sound, then go out and either turn the circuit breaker switches off and on, or unscrew and replace fuses until you hear the vacuum or radio go off. You'll know then that the circuit is controlled by the switch or fuse you just handled. Mark it with "living room", "laundry room," or whatever, then move the vacuum or radio on to another room. You can pinpoint circuits throughout your whole house that way.

WORN PLUGS

Once, many long years ago, as they say in the story books, I was an inmate in a well-known girls' finishing school. About halfway through our first year, my roommate and I discovered the plug to our radio had become worn and loose. My immediate reaction was, "Call Daddy, he'll fix it!" That had been my solution to every problem concerning broken things up to that momentous year of my life. Of course, Daddy was 1500 miles away, and *may* not have taken kindly to my plea. I'll never know, though, because that little blond dynamo who shared by room simply sat down and *fixed the thing herself*! Frankly, I was open-mouthed with awe that a *girl*, and a well-bred girl who was studying art history at that, had such knowledge. It would never have occurred to me to repair that plug myself.

I do believe that watching her make that simple repair was the first crack in the door that led me to realize I could do almost *anything* if I just tried.

Actually, repairing a worn plug *is* easy. First, you need to take a good look at it. Does it seem to be all one solid piece of rubber or plastic, with no screws, or is there open space in it? Many cords come with open spaces today. You *can't* repair that kind of plug but you can slip on a new one in about five seconds flat. General Electric makes a great replacement called a "Quick Switch Single Connector." You'll find that it looks much like the one on your cord, except that it has a little hinged flap on the back and a hole on the side. You simply cut the cord on your lamp or radio with scissors just below the old plug and push the end of the cord into the new plug through that hole. Press the flap down and...voila! Your lamp works again! What you've done is press some little prongs into the rubber-covered wire, making the connection. What could be simpler?

It's a little more difficult to repair the heavier cord on your iron, or any appliance with a heavy duty plug. This might take a long as five *minutes*. If the plug appears to be in good condition (that is, not broken and the prongs still there), but the *wires* are just frayed, you won't even need to buy a replacement.

Look closely at the plug. You may need to remove a disc of heavy paper in order to see the works inside. You'll see little brass screws on either side of the two prongs. These screws *should* have the ends of some wires wrapped tightly around them. Inside every electrical cord are *two* wires, the *hot* wire and the *ground* wire. Each wire is actually a group of many tiny copper wires. Both are necessary to make the appliance work. Most plug problems are caused when the screws either work loose, releasing those wires, or the wire finally frays away, and the screw has nothing to hold onto.

If there appears to be an inch or two of copper wire available for each screw, just loosen the screws, wrap the wires tightly around them, and tighten them down again. Be careful that the wires which you've wrapped around one screw do not touch the other screw or the wires under it. These two wires must stay separated for the cord to work properly. Put the paper disc back on and you're finished.

However, chances are that you'll find at least one of the wires too short to wrap around the screw. It has worn through with use. What you need to do, then, is loosen both screws and pull the cord completely out of the plug. Cut it off about an inch below the broken section. Now, separate those two wires from one another. If the cord is rubber covered, this separator may just involve pulling the wires apart for a couple of inches. If the cord is fabric covered, you'll need to cut the fabric before you can separate the wires.

You now need to remove about an inch of the rubber covering from each of those wires. A good sharp knife will do it quickly, but be careful that you don't cut into the wires themselves. All you want to do is expose them. If you should slip and cut the wires, too, just start over a bit below that point.

An easy way to cut the covering is to bend the wire until it's in a U shape. With your knife make a slit across the top of the bend. Turn the wire over and slit the other side of the covering. The rubber sheath over the wire will slip off easily. Do both wires this way.

Now, push both of the wires back through the hole in the plug. Separate the two wires. Wrap the full length of one of the copper sections you've exposed around a screw and tighten it. Repeat for the other wire and the other screw. Replace the paper disc. All done! If the paper disc is lost or torn, cut another one to fit from heavy paper or cardboard. You *must* have this disc on any plug that requires it, incidentally. I discovered this one day after three trips to reset a switch on my circuit breaker. Every time I plugged my iron into the outlet it would spit at me and trip the circut breaker. The plug was in good condition but the paper disc has disappeared. I just cut a new circle of cardboard from the end flap of a box of chocolate-covered cherries, pushed the prongs through it until it was tight on the plug, and ironed away!

FLUORESCENT LIGHTS THAT STALL AND FLICKER

I really don't like fluorescent lights. They're more trouble and more costly than incandescent blubs, and some of them can make your complexion look like Dracula's mother-in-law after a two-week binge.

However, if you have them, you should know how to take care of them. One of the most common problems is slow starting. You flip the switch as you go in to brush your teeth and just about the time you're finished and ready to leave for work, the thing finally comes on. This is caused, usually, by a worn-out starter. The starter is a little round gadget about the size of a dime that you'll find at the end of the fixture. Remove it and get a replacement from the hardware store. Screw it back in and you shouldn't have any more trouble.

If a fluorescent light comes on quickly but flickers almost constantly while on, the chances are it's about come to the end of the road. Take it out and replace it with a new one. You may feel a little foolish carrying the old one down to the store but I would make certain the new one is the same size and type. There are several types of fluorescent tubes and you want to be sure you get the same kind you took out.

EXTENSION CORDS

Avoid using extension cords if at all possible. But, if you absolutely *must*, follow two important rules. *Rule One:* Be sure the extension cord is the same *size* and *type* as the appliance you're using. That is, don't try to use the small size (suitable for electric hair curlers, etc.) on the room air conditioner. That takes a heavy duty wire. (See Fig. 9-1.) *Rule Two:* Don't overload the extension cord. Just because it has several lovely little places to plug appliances in doesn't mean you have to use them all. You must consider the *total wattage* of everything you attach to that cord. The National Fire Protection Association says the total should not exceed 700 watts for a regular extension cord.

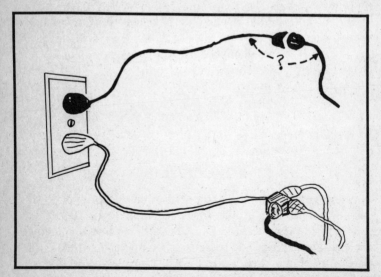

Fig. 9-1. When using extension cords make sure the cord is the same size and type as the appliance you're attaching to it, and do not overload the cord.

This chart will help you figure the average number of watts of several common appliances.

APPLIANCE	WATTS	APPLIANCE	WATTS
Clock	2	Window Fan	200
Lamp	60-150	Vacuum Cleaner	210
Radio	75	Floor Polisher	335
TV	110-315	Toaster	1130
Food Mixer	110	Broiler	1180
Electric Blanket	190	Radiant Heater	1270

As you can see, the appliances with heating coils are definite no-no's where extension cords are concerned, unless you use the heavy duty type.

Almost every electric gadget has a plate or impression somewhere on it listing the wattage it carries. My coffee pot says 1000 watts, the electric comb is 360 watts, the popcorn popper, 120 watts. I could *not* find it on the heating pad or the typewriter I'm using. But, if I wanted to estimate their wattage I would probably say the heating pad rated somewhere around 100 watts and the typewriter less than that. You can do the same in order to stay safely within the 700 watt limit.

This is important, ladies. Just ask any fireman how many times he's been called to help put out an electrical fire caused by faulty or overloaded wiring. I know it's old and corny, but the truism still fits: better safe than sorry.

10

Appliances

A Broken Toaster Can Be a Shocking Experience

Don't tell me machines are logical. So help me, I once had a Sears dryer which after years of faithful service was about ready to lurch off into that big repair shop in the sky. The starter button on the door didn't work, but it wasn't worth paying for a service call to get it fixed. The only way to start the machine was to close the door, then kick it three times in rapid succession in a certain spot near the lower right-hand side. One kick wouldn't work. Two kicks—nothing. But, on the third kick the old thing was off and roaring. I ask you, is that logical?

Now I'm not going to suggest that you crawl inside *your* dryer the next time it quits and rewind the motor or whatever those wealthy little old repair men *do* to earn their keep. But, there *are* things you can do.

WHAT TO DO BEFORE CALLING THE SERVICEMAN

First, are you *sure* the appliance needs the ministrations of a repair man? I read a report once that said at least *one-third* of all service calls (and that added up to $50,000,000 worth of wasted money) was completely unnecessary.

Here's where your feminine logic (remember, that *machine* is *not* logical) comes in. Check *everything* before you rush to the phone with a desperate plea for help, at $15 an hour. Make sure the plug is pushed all the way in, and that no fuse is blown or circuit breaker turned off (there's an explanation of these two problems in the chapter on electricity).

Are the proper buttons pushed in, out, sideways, or whatever? I had a neighbor once who struggled with a new electric range for *days* trying to get the oven to turn on. Sometimes it would, sometimes it wouldn't. Finally, the shop sent out a repairman who showed her some tiny print around a little button that said "Push for Manual." It had to be pushed *in* for her to turn the oven on herself. It was supposed to be *out* for the Time-Bake sequence. In her frantic pushing and pulling of the switches, she would sometimes have it right and sometimes have it wrong, which accounted for the fool thing's erratic behavior.

So, read the instruction booklet carefully and keep it handy for future reference. My friend had been using an electric range for years but his new one had so many fancy features that it took an engineer to understand them all. As science marches on, life becomes more complicated (though, admittedly, easier) for us button-pushers.

If the plug is in, the currrent on, switches in order, and the appliance still won't work, try a little minor housecleaning. Don't mess around with the innards of any machine or appliance. *Do* check to see if dust or grease is the problem. Those coils on the back of the refrigerator are there for a purpose, and they must have air to generate power necessary to keep your Cold Duck cold. A two-inch thick layer of dust on those coils will cut down efficiency tremendously, so clean them periodically.

That tiny flame—the pilot light—that controls many appliances also reacts poorly when its outlet hole is clogged with grease. Try wiping it off and perhaps cleaning the little hole with a tissue wrapped around a toothpick. This same trick will work on gas ranges whose burners won't light fully and on gas space heaters. I remember my father readying the heaters for use every fall by disconnecting them from the wall then *blowing* air through all the gas jets with a narrow rubber tube. This got rid of the dust which had accumulated all summer as my mother and I took our annual six months' sabbatical from housework.

NO WATER IN WASHING MACHINE

If the water won't come on in the washing machine, check behind it. You'll find two faucets on the wall, one for hot water, one for cold. Make sure they are turned on. Normally, faucets are on when they are screwed all the way counterclockwise. However, there *are* recorded instances of plumbers (and electricians and carpenters) installing things backwards, so try both ways. Would you believe that when I moved into my present house—built by a well-known builder—I discovered the electrician had installed the furnace switch upside down, and one basement window was inside out, set in solid concrete?

Check to see if the rubber hose is kinked, stopping the flow of water. Is there an overload switch which may have been tripped?

NO HEAT IN DRYER

Gas dryers require both electricity and gas to operate. If the drum turns over but it doesn't heat up, chances are that the pilot light is out. It's a good idea, incidentally, to locate this pilot light when the machine is working properly because they are sometimes ridiculously hard to find when the flame is out.

Every dryer has a little plate on it somewhere telling how to relight the pilot light. Generally, you press a button while holding a match to the pilot. It may take as long as a minute to ignite. It's a simple operation. The hardest part will be locating the place to put the match.

FURNACE THAT WON'T COME ON

Ever wake up on a frosty morning to discover it was colder *inside* the house than out? Chances are the pilot light on the furnace went out during the night. Put on your heavy coat, pick up a flashlight, some kitchen matches, and hie yourself down to the basement or wherever the furnace is housed. Look it over carefully for a metal plate with directions on relighting the pilot light. This is where you'll need the flashlight because they never put these out in plain sight. On my furnace you have to pry off a cover which conceals the workings of the furnace. But those directions are in there somewhere. They may not be too clear, either, about just where the pilot light *is*. You should find it when everything's in working order. But if you don't know where it is, or couldn't find it, just follow the directions they give about holding down the button, etc., then run a lighted kitchen match over every little part that looks feasible. Sooner or later you'll hit the right place and the pilot will catch. After you find the pilot mechanism, mark the pipes near it with a big circle in red paint or fingernail polish so you won't have so much trouble next time the thing blows out.

LOOSE SEAL ON REFRIGERATOR DOOR

That little soft rubber strip around the inside edges of your refrigerator door is called a *gasket*. Its purpose is to provide an airtight seal. As it ages, it tends to lose firmness and, consequently, its sealing power. If yours is the type with a small space between the top of the gasket and the door, you can rejuvenate it and put off replacement for many months.

Just cut long strips of cardboard approximately the width of the gasket and slip them between it and the door (Fig. 10-1). You may need two or more layers of cardboard to do the job. Dab a bit of contact cement on the back side of the gasket every six or eight inches to seal it to the cardboard.

WORN-OUT ELECTRIC BLANKET

When that cozy old electric blanket you got in college finally gives up the ghost, face the fact that it's gone. But you don't have to completely discard it. The fabric is probably still good, and plenty warm enough for spring nights, even without the aid of electricity. Locate the end of the old wires, cut a small hole in the casing holding them, and pull the wires out. Sew the hole back up, and you'll get at least another season's use from the old dear.

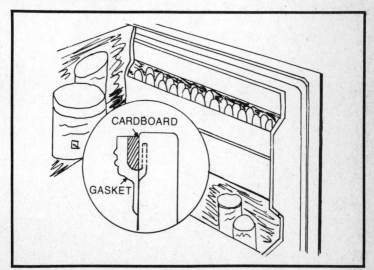

Fig. 10-1. Slipping cardboard between the gasket and the refrigerator door.

THAT BROKEN TOASTER (OR IRON, OR COFFEE POT)

Now, about that toaster. Let's face it. A girl like you has no business poking around the insides of a broken electric appliance because unless you graduated from General Electric's Repairman School (or whatever they call it), you're liable to shock yourself right into orbit and burn the house down in the bargain.

Find a good, reliable repair shop and take the appliance in for an *estimate*. Don't ever leave it with instructions, "Just fix the old thing—hang the cost!" You might want to hang *yourself* when you get the bill!

The services of repairmen are often expensive. Small appliances are often not so expensive. If the bill comes to $8.50 to get the old iron back in working order and you can buy a new one with a year's guarantee for $10.95 you'd obviously be better off buying the new one.

Always get an estimate!

OILING SMALL APPLIANCES

Almost any piece of machinery needs oiling occasionally. They'll work better and last far longer if you follow a regular schedule of lubrication. But use the right oil, please. Most small appliances and such things as window fans and sewing machines will do nicely on regular household oil. Many have a small hole specifically made for you to put in that drop or two every month. Others should have the oil dropped directly onto the moving parts. And, while you're at it, wipe away the dust and grime that has collected there.

However, on your small kitchen appliances such as mixers, can openers, etc., use a bit of plain old mineral oil instead of the household oil, which is not edible. You won't have to worry about contaminating your food that way. An eye dropper makes a good tool for applying the mineral oil, by the way.

OH, NO! A SCRATCH!

Does your lovely brick-red refrigerator (or washer, or dishwasher) have an ugly scratch right down the front of the door? *You* know the movers did it, but they said it was there all the time and you're sick, sick, sick? Well, quit fussing, and go lift a dark red crayon from the sweetest little girl you know. Rub the crayon into the scratch, then polish the excess off with a soft cloth. Go over the whole thing then with polishing wax and no one will ever know the difference.

Eek !
A Mouse !

**How to Get Rid of Mice,
Ants, Roaches, Termites, and Other
Uninvited Guests**

I'd be the last one to tell you that *every* home can be entirely varmint-free because I know it isn't so. In most parts of the country, however, you can control unwanted insect and rodent guests to a large extent. Good housekeeping and the right pesticide are the secrets.

Let's take these pests one at a time.

MICE

What attracts mice to your home? Open garbage cans, stacked firewood, and utidy alleyways are three of the most common come-ons for the little varmints. How do they get *inside*? They crawl in through open or unscreened doors, windows, ventilators, and through holes around electrical inlets or pipes. And, although this may convert you to a canned-food addict, occasionally we *carry* them into our homes in sacks of fresh potatoes and other produce we buy at that antiseptic supermarket on the corner.

If you suspect (or know!) you have mice, follow these recommendations from the U.S. Department of the Interior. They're proven methods for control.

1. *Starve them out*. Keep your garbage cans tightly closed. Store food in glass or plastic containers with

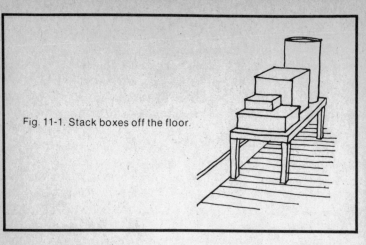

Fig. 11-1. Stack boxes off the floor.

tightly fitting lids. Keep your home as clean and free from sources of food for them as possible.

2. *Remove their shelter*. Store boxes, out-of-season equipment, and all that junk you're saving for a garage sale someday on tables or shelves several inches off the floor (Fig. 11-1). Keep the basement or storage room clear of litter. Don't stack wood for your fireplace against the house walls (Fig. 11-2).

3. *Build them out*. Nail closely spaced wire mesh over ventilators. Keep floor drains tightly fastened down (Fig. 11-3). Make (or have made) closely fitting metal collars to fit around all openings for pipe or wiring into

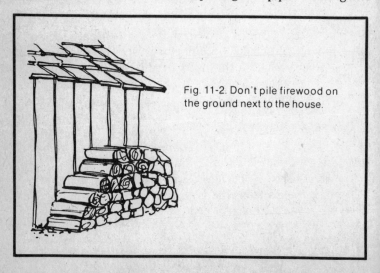

Fig. 11-2. Don't pile firewood on the ground next to the house.

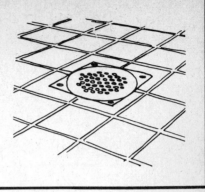

Fig. 11-3. Make sure drains fit tightly.

the house (Fig. 11-4). Install good springs on your doors so they'll close securely.

4. *Exterminate the ones who make it in.* Get 10 to 12 old-fashioned wooden-base snap traps and place them along the walls behind the refrigerator, the range, furniture, etc., in such a way that the mice must cross them. Bait the traps with peanut butter mixed with uncooked oatmeal, bacon, gumdrops, or raisins. Now some mice are pretty nimble and can pick the goodies right off the trigger, then scamper away scot-free with a meal at your expense. Be smarter than they are. Just enlarge the trigger by hooking a small square of cardboard under the trigger's sharp prong, before placing the bait on the prong (Fig. 11-5). They'll have to step on the

Fig. 11-4. Fit collars around openings for pipes or wires.

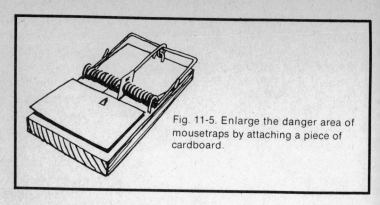

Fig. 11-5. Enlarge the danger area of mousetraps by attaching a piece of cardboard.

cardboard to get to the food—and the pressure of that step will spring the trap.

There are poisons available, of course. But, don't use them unless the mice are simply taking over. They're dangerous to children and pets.

ANTS

Ants are one of the easiest household insects to control. The don't scurry away when you get near and they don't fly off into the next room the minute you pick up a swatter.

One of the most effective ant control devices is a strong pesticide used with *care*. It'll quickly kill the ants you see and prevent re-infestation for at least two or three months. You can buy these pesticides at the hardware or drug store under a variety of trade names.

If ants aren't too bad at your house, and all you see is an occasional queue winding along the kitchen window sill, I'd say stick with the handy aerosol bombs. There are several made by well-known firms on the market, and they're quite adequate for small jobs. But, if you're afraid to walk bare-footed across the floor for fear of getting stung, (Fig. 11-6) or if you have nightmares about giant ant-like creatures crushing you house to dust with their slow plodding, then get one of the stronger pesticides.

One of the ready-mixed oil sprays is what you want to use inside the house. It dries to an almost invisible film and will last and last, prolonging protection for weeks after the first application.

Trace the ants along their parade, spraying all the way back to the point that they disappear under a baseboard, through a cabinet, or what-have-you. Shoot some of the spray in all the cracks and crevices in that general area. If the ants are nesting inside the house, your dousing will probably discourage them from coming out again.

But, go outside the house and check the foundation of the house in that general area, anyway. You just *may* see a swarm of ants scurrying along the walls. If that's the case, they are probably nesting outside, and wandering inside for supper and a warm bed.

You can spray the exterior walls with a two percent oil-base spray. Or get the granule type which is sprinkled dry on the ground along the foundation, around supporting pillars, and into their hills.

A combination of indoor and outdoor applications will control ants before they have a chance to get onto your table or into your sugar bowl again.

But, just plain good housekeeping is an excellent barrier to ant trouble. Keep the floor clean of spilled food, vacuum regularly, and keep your food containers closed.

COCKROACHES

Ugh! Is anything more repulsive than to walk into your kitchen at night, turn on the light, and see a fleet of cockroaches scurrying for cover? I'm not going to tell you that getting *rid* of cockroaches is easy. I know better. But, unless you live in one of the very warm and damp parts of our country, you can *control* the pests with good sanitation and the right pesticide.

The first step toward eliminating an infestation of cockroaches is to keep your home as clean and well-aired as possible. The second is to begin a regular program of spraying and dusting with any one of several good insecticides. Diazinon, Lindane, Ronnel, and Malathion are all good if used

Fig. 11-6. Large lines of lots of ants calls for strong, prompt action.

with care. They'll all kill the insect on contact and leave a residue which will kill any of his friends who amble in during the next few weeks.

Roaches can develop an immunity to certain pesticides, and I suggest you check with the county agent or a reliable dealer before you decide which to buy. He'll know the most effective type and brand for your area. Unless the infestation is very heavy, use only a liquid insecticide inside your home. Dusts sometimes float through the air and can contaminate your food and coat your dishes. However, if you've moved into a house that's absolutely overrun with the little beasts, use a combination of dust (it can be puffed into crevices a spray won't reach) and spray until they begin to retreat.

Use an ordinary household plunger-type sprayer that produces a coarse spray to wet down the surfaces you're treating. You don't want a fine mist for the same reason dust is undesirable—it lands on everything in sight. Many people use a small paint brush to literally paint the pesticide onto cracks and crevices. This is probably the most economical way to use your liquid pesticide, too.

Concentrate on those dark, hidden spots where roaches hide and deposit their eggs—underneath the sink and drainboard, in cracks in the cupboards and cabinets, around pipes or conduits where they pass along the wall or go through it. Don't miss the motor compartment of the refrigerator, behind window and door frames, behind loose baseboards and in radio and television cabinets. Coat the undersides of tables and chairs and behind mirrors. I wouldn't advise spraying directly onto good books, but you can paint a border of the pesticide along the edges of all your bookshelves.

Be sure to remove all food, dishes, and shelf paper before you spray into your kitchen cupboards and the pantry. Cover the shelves with new paper after the spray has dried, and before you put the cornflakes and grandmother's best Wild Rose china back.

It isn't necessary to spray inside drawers if you treat the sides, back, and undersurfaces. Just be sure you keep them clean.

There are baits on the market which are effective in cockroach control, but they are also poisonous to children and pets. Think twice about using them.

Sprays and dusts will kill those insects already in the house, and for a few weeks will kill those that come in contact

136

with treated surfaces. They will *not* prevent more insects from entering the house. You can make it as hard as possible for more insects to enter, though, by sealing all cracks, and crevices around door, windows, and pipes with caulking compound (see the chapter on the outdoors). The reason older homes are so often infested with cockroaches is that they have so many openings into the house, from settling, rot, poor construction, etc. The more of these openings you close, the more pest-free your home will be.

HOUSE FLIES

House flies normally breed outdoors in decaying organic matter. They are notorious carriers of disease and filth and every effort should be made to keep them off the food and serving surfaces of the home.

The place to start is outdoors, where they breed. Keep the yard free of that decaying organic matter. Make sure all garbage cans have tight-fitting lids. Treat those cans with a surface spray (one whose effect is long lasting) to discourage flies from using it as a landing field and nursery. Then, screen your windows and doors, and keep those screens in good repair. (There's a discussion on screen repair in the chapter on doors and windows.)

Finally, buy an aerosol spray especially intended for flying insects and use it whenever you find those flies buzzing around in spite of all your precautions. I've found the most effective way to use the spray is to close the house up, then go from room to room, filling the air with the mist from the aerosol bomb. As a room becomes fogged, I close that room's door and move to the next room. I eventually work myself right out the back door, shut it, then take off for the pool for an hour or so.

Only a giant fly out of a horror movie could survive *that* treatment!

MOSQUITOES

My earliest memory concerning medicine is the little vial of quinine pills I had to force down daily (they were huge!) because of a mild attack of malaria.

Fortunately, with modern insecticides and community fogging efforts, mosquito-carried malaria is almost a thing of the past. But, the vicious insects still hurt or itch like crazy when they bite, and can ruin your good looks if you have to spend too many nights up chasing one around the room with a fly swatter instead of getting your beauty sleep.

Controlling mosquitoes in the home involves much the same treatment as controlling flies. Screen your windows and fog the place thoroughly when you find they've invaded your privacy. In addition, change the water in flower vases frequently. Standing water is a favorite breeding spot for mosquito larvae and they aren't the least bit particular whether it's outdoors in a ditch or in a cut crystal vase full of gladiola blossoms.

Watch the water you keep in saucers under house plants, too. Don't just add to it every day or so. Pour out the old water, rinse the saucer, then pour in a fresh supply.

It's also helpful to use a good surface spray (one with a residual effect which will stick to the surface treated). Malathion or fenthion sprays are both good. Use your household sprayer to moisten the underside of furniture, under beds, in closets—any dark, secluded spot where mosquitoes lay their eggs. A good application should last for several weeks.

WASPS, HORNETS, YELLOW JACKETS, MUD DAUBERS

If you've ever been bitten by a wasp, you know their nests should *not* be allowed to remain hanging there on the eaves of your house. The bite is extremely painful, and under certain circumstances, can be fatal.

Go out on a dry, still night and spray those nests thoroughly with Dichlorvos or something equivalent. You should protect yourself with a long-sleeved jacket, gloves, and some sort of protection over your face in case any of the pests take a notion to divebomb you before you hit the dust.

You may have to stand on a ladder in order to get the spray well up on these nests. I'd suggest having a friend along to steady the ladder because it would be easy to lose your balance and fall, in case that little beastie *did* attack and you ducked. There's no point in avoiding wasp stings just to end up with a broken leg!

TERMITES

I have a friend who was prettying her dining room for a party one day when, while giving the carpet a quick last-minute glance, she noticed that something was wrong with the *baseboards*. They just didn't look right. She got down on her hands and knees, black chiffon and all, and stared open-mouthed with horror. There was nothing left of the baseboards but varnish!

Termites had literally eaten their way into her dining room, chewing up every scrap of wood in the baseboards, but foregoing the varnish as dessert. This was an old house, and the baseboards had been varnished and re-varnished for so many years that the coating was thick enough to stand alone after the little varmints got through with their destruction.

She went on with the party but, frankly, was on edge the whole evening—she was afraid the floor was going to cave in under her guests any minute. For all she knew, the floor was eaten through, too, and there was nothing supporting the dining table except her precious oriental rug!

The best protection against termites is a well-built home. And the next time you build one, insist on pressure-treated sills and joists, and a poured foundation, or a monolithic concrete slab.

But since you probably don't intend to rush out and hire a contractor today any more than I do, let's talk about the things you can do to prevent termites in the home you now have.

First, know what they look like. Termites are often mistaken for ants, or flying ants, and vice versa. Look carefully at the next ant that walks by. You'll see he has a

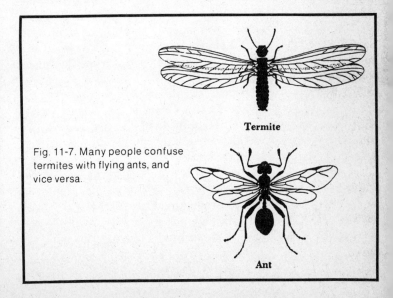

Termite

Fig. 11-7. Many people confuse termites with flying ants, and vice versa.

Ant

characteristically thin waist. If he's a winged ant, his wings will be of unequal size and will be transparent (Fig. 11-7).

Termites aren't nearly so graceful. Adult worker termites, the ones who do the damage, are wingless and grayish white in color. The reproductive, or sexual adults, have yellow-brown to black bodies and two pairs of long, whitish, opaque wings of equal size. Both types have thick, pudgy waists.

The first sign of a termite infestation is often a swarming of these winged insects from the basement area of a building, or discarded wings lying on the ground or floor beneath doors and windows, or those long earthen tubes snaking up the foundation of the house.

If you live in southern Florida or along the coast of California your home is subject to invasion by drywood termites. They don't require contact with the soil at all, and you'll know you have them if you find neat little cavities cut across the grain of comparatively solid wood. Termites leave compressed pellets along their trail in those cavities and occasionally will push one out onto the ground below. The poisons necessary to kill termites are too potent for you to handle. If you suspect you have an infestation, call a good exterminator.

With luck, you won't have termites at all. But, termites infest every state in this nation, and it will pay you to practice good termite preventive measures. Remove all dead wood from around the house foundations. This means stumps, roots, piles of old lumber, and fireplace wood. Burn or haul away what you don't need. Stack useful lumber and firewood in a well-ventilated place, off the ground, away from the house. Provide as much ventilation as possible in the crawl space under the house. Termites *hate* light and sunshine.

Don't allow moisture to stand around the foundations of the house. If your lot is poorly drained, get someone with a grader to come in and slope it so rainwater drains away from the house. Termites *love* dampness.

Remove any wooden trellises which touch the ground and replace them with metal ones. Finally, take a few minutes every month or so to walk around the house and make a *visual* inspection. If you live in a high-danger area, termite-wise, it will pay to have a *professional* inspection once a year, too.

12

Protection From Theft and Attack

A Burglar-Proof Home Is Very Good For the Nerves!

There is no such thing as absolute protection from theft or assault for the woman living alone, or anyone else for that matter. But, by using a double-barreled approach to safety (*not* a double-barreled shotgun, please! You might shoot off you toes!), you can make the possibility of theft or assault highly improbable. The two barrels are: common sense and the proper mechanical devices.

There is no need for fear living alone. Millions of women do it, and manage very well. But you should know a few basic rules. Let's take our categories one at a time.

FOILING THE CAT BURGLAR

One of the leading magazines carried an article not long ago about burglar-proofing the home. It was written by a reformed thief who had spent 23 years in prison before deciding the straight life was more profitable, hour for hour. In the article he told exactly how we naive bunnies made it so easy for him to, as he said, "live better than a movie star," on the pickings of a few hour's work each evening.

Did you know a prowler, such as our expert once was, enters a home in this country every fifteen seconds? And, daytime burglaries are up almost 300 percent in some areas? How, in a nation so well policed as ours, is this possible? Listen to the expert.

There are three things which all burglars fear—*lights*, *noise*, and *curious neighbors*. Most of us think that leaving a light on in the hallway and another on the front porch will deter a burglar. Actually, this just broadcasts the fact that we've gone out for the evening. Most homes use a great deal more light than that when the owner is home. The experienced burglar, when he sees a poorly lit house, will cautiously check out a few more telltale signs. He'll peek into the garage to see if the car is out. Keep those garage doors shut at all times! If there is a window in the garage, block it out. The sight of an empty garage is like an engraved invitation to a thief looking for an empty house.

Our thief may walk around the house, peering into windows for signs of activity. (Keep those drapes drawn at night!) He'll listen carefully because most inhabited homes have some *sounds* in them. (Leave the radio on!)

Incidentally, burglars are most active between the hours of seven in the evening and midnight—the time of day when many people are away from their homes.

If you want to use light for a deterrent, use lots of it. It's the most inexpensive method available to keep burglars at a distance. Did you know you can burn a 50-watt bulb *all evening* for just a penny or two? That's cheap insurance any way you look at it.

Leave several lights on in the house. Turn on the lights at *all* exterior doors, and if you have floodlamps, flick them on, too. Burglars usually enter a home from a concealed back or side entrance. They practically never go in the front door!

Those timing devices that turn the lights on and off at a certain time are a good investment, too. They can save you from having to walk into a dark house if you've been away all day, and can be set to turn your lights off and on every evening while you're away on vacation. Try plugging your radio into the timer, too. Tuned to a talk station, the radio's low chatter can give the impression that someone is home.

More about noise: man's best friend can also be woman's best protection. A good, barking dog will scare off almost any burglar. Although Rover may be fourteen years old, on Pablum because his teeth fell out years ago, and wouldn't know what to do with a burglar if he caught one, his barking is enough to send most of them scurrying. Burglars don't know he's harmless. If he *sounds* ferocious, that's enough. His bark will alert you that something is amiss, giving you time to dial the police or reach for that switch that lights up the yard like the proverbial Christmas tree.

Burglar alarm systems are the other big noisemakers. Within certain limitations, they are effective. When tripped, they make a racket that will shoot you out of bed and let the whole neighborhood know there's a prowler at your place. There are dozens of different models on the market, ranging from a transistorized unit especially designed for apartment dwellers, which sells for about $39.95, to custom-designed systems costing thousands of dollars.

Our ex-burglar expert, though, says that those little signs which some people proudly tack up saying, "Warning! This Home Protected By Never-Snooze Burglar Alarm System" are worse than useless. They actually tip the careful thief that he should locate the circuit breaker box and switch off the house current before attempting an entry. Some burglars take this precaution as a matter of course, anyway, just in case there is an electrically controlled alarm system installed in the house.

Even worse, that gentleman of the night may figure that if you're going to all the expense of a burglar alarm system you must have some goodies of real value lying around, and he may decide yours is the house to concentrate his talents on.

Some authorities advise using a battery-powered alarm system which will ring even if the house current is turned off. This makes sense to me. Not many of us, though, have burglar alarm systems. And, according to many police officials, the best all-around, 24-hour-a-day protection you can give your home is simply good locks on every door and window.

Let's take a little test right now. We're going to see just how quickly and easily a burglar could open your front door without breaking in and without making a sound.

Get a credit card from your wallet. Go outside and insert it between the locked front door and the jamb, right at the lock. Push the card against the spring lock. Try to slide the card through the crack, pushing the lock back into the door as you go. If it passes the lock, simply take hold of the door handle and pull. The door will come open.

Did it work on your door? Not all doors will open this way, but you'd be surprised how many do. I know of one case where a team of burglars, dressed as moving men, pulled a large van up to the door of a motel room of one of this country's leading chains and literally cleaned the place out, right down to the soap dishes in the bathroom! How did they get into the locked room? Simple. With a thin strip of plastic, much like your credit card.

The answer to such nervy characters is to have dead-bolt locks installed on all your first floor doors. The credit card trick will not work on them, and they are exceedingly hard to tamper with. Each dead-bolt lock will cost you abut $20 installed. If you live in an apartment the manager should be willing to go at least halves with you on the cost.

Those sliding glass patio doors are duck soup for the average burglar. The locks are a breeze to pick and many can be lifted right up and out of the track by a man who knows his stuff. You can foil him, though, if you have an electric drill. Close the doors completely. You'll see that the metal frame of one section is directly behind the metal frame of the other section, in the center of the opening. Working from the *inside*, carefully drill straight through the frame closet to you. Continue drilling through *one* side of the other frame. *Do not drill all the way through to the outside*.

Now, get a big, heavy nail that will fit into that hole. At night, or when you plan to be away, just stick the spike into the hole you drilled. The door cannot be lifted or moved with that nail in place. It's a simple step, but effective.

If your lease won't allow any alterations to the patio door (the Scrooges!), you can still rig up a fairly good burglar foiler with a broomstick. Close the door completely and measure the distance along the track from the edge of the movable section's frame to the end of the track. Cut your broomstick (or a sturdy dowel from the lumber company) to fit this measurement exactly. It must be a tight fit. Place the stick on the track with one end touching the stationary frame and the other end against the movable door frame. With the stick in place it will be *very* difficult for the door to be opened or lifted from the outside, even if the lock is picked.

Most homes are cased by the clever burglar long before they are actually entered. Some burglars make a practice of looking for homes where the occupants are obviously on vacation. So, the next time you take off for Acapulco, be sure you follow a few simple precautions before you leave. Naturally, you'll stop the mail, milk, and paper deliveries.

Also, hire a neighborhood boy to mow the lawn and pick up circulars, and pay him in advance. Get a timer and set it to turn a few lamps and the radio on at dusk and off at your regular bedtime. And, tell the police and the neighbors how long you plan to be away. They'll gladly keep an eye on the place for you.

Some thieves specialize in "house calls." They come to your door in broad daylight posing as salesmen, meter readers, deliverymen. Anything at all to get inside and find out where you keep the sterling silver. Some will come to the door asking to use the phone, "for just a minute." Well, that minute is all they need to note that you have a color television set in the living room, and a good camera in the bookcase, a fur coat hanging in the front closet, and an electric typewriter on the desk. It's plenty of time to make mental notes on the best entry into the home, quick exits, and how easily the doors can be seen by the neighbors.

You may feel ungracious refusing to let a little old gray-haired lady in to call the local garage for a tow truck because her car just went off a fifty-foot embankment. But, more than one grandmotherly type has turned out to be the brains behind a ring of thieves. Just offer to make the call for her. Never let *anyone* in who doesn't have the proper credentials.

Oh, one last word of caution. Please be creative when you hide your crown jewels at home! Our ex-burglar friend says the very first place a thief looks after he enters a home is the right-hand side of the third drawer of the bedroom dresser. It seems that's where all we ladies tend to stash our baubles. I blushed with shame at being so ordinary when I read that, because that is exactly where my little velvet box was hidden!

It is much better, according to the man who should know, to hollow out a book for your pretties and file it away on the top shelf between *Portnoy's Complaint* and *The Sensuous Woman*. Or drop them into a plastic bag which can be tucked away at the bottom of a box of corn flakes. Or burrow a hole in your wig stand. Most burglars allow themselves only three or four minutes to complete a job and if they have to take the place apart looking for your little cache, they'll give up and move on to the next house on their list. Don't take a chance on donating your lovely trinkets to the Burglar's Local #127 Retirement Fund. Use your feminine ingenuity and concoct a hiding place no mere man would ever dream of. Help stamp out crime!

THINK AHEAD—AND YOU'LL ARRIVE HOME SAFELY

A policewoman in one of our most troubled cities says, "Most assaults on women are not planned, but rather are the result of opportunity."

Some women unconsciously invite attack by wearing the wrong clothes at the wrong place at the wrong time. Super-skimpy clothing on the beach is normal and seldom provokes anything more than an admiring glance. The same outfit on dry land is an RSVP for trouble. The smart woman, when walking alone, wears conservative, inconspicuous clothing. You may be as proud as punch of that golden suntan and size seven figure (and I don't blame you!), but save the show for a time when there's someone you *know* to admire it.

One of the most enlightened companies I know of provides taxies, at no cost, for its women employees who leave work at 2 a.m. The women are picked up at the entrance to the building and taken straight home. Because of this sensible policy, the company has no trouble finding people to work that awful shift. If you work nights, you might mention this to your boss. It could be one of the best fringe benefits you ever received.

If you must walk alone at night, walk against the traffic, and avoid alleyways, tall shubbery, and dark buildings. Walk near the curb and near lights (Fig. 12-1). Walk briskly as though you are headed someplace and someone is expecting you. *Do not loiter or windowshop.* You might give the impression you're there for a different purpose.

If you should be approached by someone in an automobile, turn and run in the opposite direction from which it is coming, and don't stop until you reach a policeman, an open business, or a lighted home. It doesn't matter whose home it is. Try the front door. If it's open, run in. If it's locked, stand there and yell loud and clear, "I'm home, Dad, open the door." The chances are your would-be attacker will disappear. No matter what, *never* get in that car, even if the driver has a gun. It's incredibly hard for him to hit a moving target. Outside the car, you have chance at safety.

Never carry large amounts of money in your purse. You won't be tempted to fight for it (and make the purse-snatcher fight back) if there's only a dollar or two in your wallet instead of the rent money.

If someone grabs you and you can't break loose to run, fight back like the tigress that's buried in all of us. Jab your

Fig. 12-1. If you must walk home alone late at night, walk near lights, against traffic, and avoid alleyways, tall shrubbery, and dark buildings. Walk briskly as though you are headed somewhere and someone is expecting you.

fingers in his eyes, bite his hand—hard—stick an umbrella into his mid-section, slam you knee into his groin. If he grabs you from behind, catch his little fingers and bend them backwards until he lets go or they break. Grind your high heels into his instep. Batter his face with your head. This is no time to be a lady. Use *any* method you can think of to make him loosen his grip. And, above all, *scream* loud and clear. This can be your best weapon because it draws attention to you, which is the last thing an attacker wants.

Laws vary from state to state as to what you can carry in your purse for self-defense, but most policemen advise women against carrying handguns. There's too much danger of an attacker taking it away and using it on you.

Check with your own police department to see what's legal to carry on the person for self-defense in your state. With luck, you'll be allowed to use one of the many mechanical or aerosol devices on the market today. There are miniature battery-operated alarms which can be heard for blocks, aerosol cylinders of a Mace-like chemical, and good, loud whistles which are inexpensive, but very effective. A can of plain red pepper flung in the eyes has discouraged more than one mugger!

If you must be out alone at night frequently, you might look into one of the classes for women on self-defense. I once saw an average-sized, middle-aged woman throw her six-foot-tall son flat on this back on the living room rug as homework for her judo class! He went and took a few lessons himself after that!

Just remember, the best defense is a good offense. That means, use your basic intelligence to avoid dangerous situations whenever possible.

ALONE IN YOUR AUTOMOBILE

The American Automobile Association says that crimes against women involving automobiles are nearly always crimes of chance. They're a combination of time, place, and opportunity. As an intelligent woman, it behooves you to keep that combination from rolling onto the table.

First, keep the gas tank reasonably well filled at all times, and have periodic checkups to keep the car in good running order. Regular servicing is far less expensive than a major breakdown which could occur when you're halfway from here to nowhere on a lonely road at night.

This happened to me once, and made a believer of me mighty fast! I was working on a job that required some travel to neighboring towns at night. Coming home one morning at about 1 a.m., I was driving along the only road between a little college town and my village—thirty miles of narrow, winding road with only the moon to break the darkness. Suddenly, with no warning, the whole electrical system of the car quit. There I was...no lights, no horn, no flasher, no power, no *nothing*. Just me and the big, cold black night. I got out and put the hood up because I knew this was always the first thing anyone did in an emergency. Then I just stood there and stared at the motor. This was before I had taken the course in Auto Mechanics for Women. I hadn't the foggiest idea what to do after raising the hood.

It was bitterly cold. The wind was blowing. I was scared. Was I going to freeze to death out there like so many of the pioneers who had tried to populate the Rocky Mountains before central heating? Then, out of the darkenss, a car roared up and pulled up behind me. I figured it was the end, and my life began flashing before my eyes. About the time I got to the Senior Prom, I realized the gentleman approaching me had on a uniform—the beautiful, faultlessly tailored garb of a highway patrolman. Have you ever wanted to kiss a policeman? If I hadn't been completely immobilized from cold and fright, believe me, that gorgeous specimen would have gotten one right then and there. Anyway, he got out some tools and in a few minutes had my little green bomb purring again.

I found out the next day at the garage (right after I'd called in and quit the job—I didn't like it anyway) that the problem was a minor thing that could have been avoided if I'd slowed down long enough to have the car serviced.

If you ever do happen to find yourself in that scary situation, though, *don't* lock yourself in your car—window glass is easy to smash if someone is determined to do so. Leave the car's hood raised to indicate there is trouble afoot, and then *hide*—and I mean HIDE—nearby in the bushes or whatever is available. Be very, very choosy about revealing yourself if anyone stops to investigate. Ideally you should either wait till a policeman arrives or wait until daylight and then hike to the nearest house or town. Better to be cold, tired, and uncomfortable than to take a bad gamble on someone who might look innocent to you when you're desperate for help.

Better yet, listen to one who's been there: keep your car in good shape.

A few short bits of advice and then we'll get off this gloomy subject: If you find yourself being followed, don't head for home. That just tells your follower where you live, and it could open the door to real trouble. Drive until you find a police station, a well-lit gas station, or a fire station. You'll always get help there.

If a car blocks your path, stay in the *locked* car and *sit on the horn*. Avoid dark, lonely streets, if possible, and keep your doors locked at all times.

Park only in attended, commercial lots or on well-lit streets. When you return to your car do not enter it if you notice an unsavory character loitering nearby. Walk on until you can get some reliable company to stand by while you get in. And, check that back seat floor. It's the favorite hiding place for any hoodlum who plans to attack you once you get on the road.

If someone jumps into your car, do *anything* to attract attention. Run into another car, drive up on the sidewalk, make a U-turn in traffic. You want all the attention you can get. If someone is attempting to get into your car, police say forget the rules and take off—even if it means running a red light, exceeding the speed limit, or grazing another car.

If all the cautions in this chapter are making you a little paranoic, relax. The chances of your being burglarized or attacked are as slim as a fashion model if you just use your common sense and avoid potentially dangerous situations.

13

The Automobile

How To Keep It Going So You'll Keep Going

Have you ever considered taking one of those automobile repair classes? They're being offered by adult education departments and the AAA in many cities to teach us how to understand our cars a little better, and how to cope with some of the inevitable emergencies that come up.

You just might, one of these days, have to take care of that loose battery cable or flooded carburetor yourself—and you can, with the proper instruction. I strongly recommend taking these courses. They're often taught by the same men who teach other men to become garage mechanics, but they begin with the usually valid assumption that you think piston rings come from the jewelry store and a vapor lock is something to keep out ghostly intruders.

I took one course in an adult education program a couple of years ago. Our class consisted of nine women ranging from a dewy-eyed bride of 19 whose husband was in the service, to a live wire on the shady side of forty who rode her own motorcycle to class and was learning to pilot a plane!

One charmer, a teacher, literally didn't know where the gas went in her car when she enrolled. By the time we finished, she was not only saving three dollars every month by filling her own tank at the self-service stations, but was able to change a flat tire and put in that extra quart of oil between changes.

My proudest moment was when I was able to sail smugly into my local garage and say, "My ignition isn't firing properly. Would you please check to see if the distributor cap is cracked?" Would you believe I was right? Me, the neighborhood featherhead, the slightly worn-around-the-edges Southern belle who wouldn't have known a distributor cap from a hole in the ground before taking the class.

One of the biggest advantages of these courses is that you gain at least a layman's knowledge of what goes on under the hood of your car. You may not be able to change the points yourself, but you will know when they need replacing. And, because you are knowledgeable about your car, you won't be such a pushover for unscrupulous garage and service station mechanics.

Our instructor told us that there were a couple of garages in our neighborhood which refused to service the cars of women who had taken the course. These con men weren't able to give the graduates a song and dance about the car needing $239 worth of work when a $25 tune-up and a carburetor adjustment would make it run like a Georgia congressman two days before election.

If your county doesn't offer a course in auto mechanics for women, go to your superintendent of schools, and tell him you have it from the highest authority (that's me) that these classes are saving money, time, and temper tantrums for the gentler sex in every *enlightened* school district in the country. If he's too archaic to see the light, then go to his wife. That ought to do it.

I could tell a dozen stories of women being duped because they literally didn't know the first thing about the mechanics of their cars. In fact, my car, years ago, developed a ghastly clanking noise on a holiday drive through the mountains. I pulled into a small service station and described the noise to the owner/mechanic. He drove the car around the block, put it up on the rack, shook his head gravely, and informed me I had a worn universal joint that would break any minute. Helplessly, I told him to fix it.

This good Samaritan then told me it would take at least two days to complete the job since he had to drive to some place that sounded like it was on the far boundaries of Afghanistan to get parts. Luckily for me, he just happened to also own a three-cell motel and greasy spoon next door where I could loll around in surely unaccustomed luxury while he ministered to my ailing automobile.

Well, I had to be at work a hundred miles away the next morning, so I refused his kind offer, got in the car, and started noisily creeping down the road, expecting the worst any minute. I had wild visions of me and my little old Firebird hurtling over cliffs, uprooting giant pine trees, and rearranging fifty-ton boulders if the universal joint, whatever that was, should suddenly give way.

Hours later, practically a basket case, I crept into my service station. In three minutes flat, the knight of the whirling digits had the trouble in the palm of his hand—five little pebbles that had somehow worked their way under a hub cap were clunking around harmlessly with every turn of the wheel. There wasn't a cotton-picking thing wrong with the universal joint. And this experience is *far* from being an unusual one. So be very wary of a dire diagnosis you get from strange mechanics:

Did you know that at least one-third of the huge sums we spend on repairs to our automobile are either for grossly padded bills or for repairs that were absolutely unnecessary in the first place? (This is a national average. I'd be willing to bet my Easter bonnet that the figure is twice that for women, especially single women.) This information comes from one of the country's leading economists and should make you think two or three times before you take that tin lizzie in for new bearings or shock absorbers again.

This isn't to say you shouldn't have necessary work done on your car. It's just a warning to be highly suspicious of *any* garage before you get in its clutches. Unfortunately, being a woman makes you seem like fair game to many auto mechanics today. A little knowledge and some advance planning, though, can help you foil these highway robbers.

Shop for an honest garage *before* you need it. Check around the neighborhood and get the names of several garages or service stations that have a decent reputation. Go to them yourself and ask their policy about payments (some won't release the car until the bill is paid in full, some demand financing at their own rates, some will accept bank financing). Find out how long they've been in business there. Using your intuition, pick a couple that impress you as being reasonably honest and seem to have enough experience behind them to be able to fix your car right the first time. See if a mechanic is normally on duty on weekends. Then explain that you don't need their services *then* but when the occasion arises, you'll give them a crack at your business. If you are satisfied with price and performance, you'll then be a regular customer. Act as though you know what you're talking about and you'll stand a better chance of getting a fair deal.

You'll probably have three main alternatives when shopping for a garage—the repair shop of the new car dealer that handles your brand of car, the service station on the corner, and a shop which does only mechanical work. Each has certain advantages. The car dealer will understand your car's peculiarities and may work at a decent price, hoping to sell you a car next time around. The service station on the corner is convenient—and open long hours. The independent mechanic has to depend on his reputation as a mechanic only—since he doesn't sell cars or gas—to stay in business, and will probably do excellent work. You just have to use your own judgment as to which will be better for you.

When the time does come that your car needs repair work, try to get at least two estimates on the final cost. If possible, take along someone who knows what the mechanic will be talking about. It seems hard to bluff a 6′4″ ex-Marine. Then, when you decide on a garage to do the work, get that estimate *in writing*. *Never* accept a cheery, "Don't worry, lady, this can't run more than $15." Make it clear that if, after getting into the car, they think the bill will run higher than the estimate, you are to be consulted before the work is done.

Also, always ask that they save the old parts for you. You may feel a little cheap doing this but it's at least a minor deterrent to their saying you owe them $39.95 for a new water pump when the old one is still in there.

Better still, if you can, hang around and *watch* them work. Say you don't have any transportation until your car is fixed, or that your brother is a hot-shot mechanic in the Army and you want to be able to discuss his work intelligently when he gets home, or that you're making a time-study survey for your night class in economics. You'll get a few dirty looks from the boys in the back, but they won't be able to charge you for four hours labor, at $12 an hour, when you were only there 45 minutes.

The main thing to remember is that at a garage you're in enemy territory, and it's legal to use any weapon in your arsenal to get your money's worth.

Finally, if you're the political type, work—through your local party's organization or through letters to your congressman—to get auto mechanics licensed by the government. Downright fraud would stop or be deterred if each auto mechanic were required to obtain a government license.

Now, let's get to work on the things *you* can do to keep your car shiny and in good running order.

SCRATCHED PAINT

What with those $50 to $100 deductible clauses in our insurance policies, we often let very minor body damage go unrepaired simply for economy. Sometimes, however, minor scratches can lead to major rust problems later on. I'm not advocating that you take up body and fender work, but you *can* get rid of that little scratch you put in the door paint.

It's easily camouflaged with touch-up paint from the auto parts store. The store will have little bottles labeled as to make and year, so if yours is a fairly recent model you can probably get matching paint. Just brush it across the scratch and the damage will be practically invisible.

If the store doesn't have your color, check out the pigtail and pinafore set in your neighborhood until you find a child with one of those giant boxes of crayons—the ones with about 98 different colors. Bribe her with an ice cream cone and borrow the crayon that comes closest in color to your car. Rub the crayon firmly into the scratch until the wax fills the groove. Wait a few minutes for the crayon wax to set, then buff it and polish with a good car wax. Fantastic!

WORN TIRES

Those four rubber tires are expensive, so it'll pay you to learn what causes them to wear prematurely. Get in the habit of inspecting the tread regularly. Ideally, the rubber should wear evenly across the surface of the tire. If it doesn't, then you have a sure sign that something needs to be adjusted.

There's one problem called *toe in* and *toe out* which happens when your wheels need realigning (or, in simple language, straightening up). You'll notice this when one side of a tire is worn smooth while the tread on the opposite side is as good as new. You may also have felt a pulling on the steering wheel to one side or the other. If this condition is left too long, unaligned wheels can actually cause a blowout when the rubber wears too thin on one side. Realignment is not expensive and is good insurance against accident or against having to replace a tire months before it's necessary.

If the tires are worn on both sides, but the center is still in good condition, then they're underinflated. Conversely, if your tires are as smooth as an insurance salesman's pitch in the center and good on the outside, then they've been overinflated.

There is an air pressure recommended for every tire. Learn what yours is and make sure the pressure is kept at that level. It's a free service at your service station and takes only a moment to check.

Even tires in excellent condition should be rotated every six months or so to keep them that way. This includes the spare, too. A good time to have it done is when you put on or remove your snow tires, or have a tire replaced. It saves your time that way.

FLAT TIRE

The surest way to avoid having to change a flat yourself is to be able to do it. If you just sit there in your car, hoping the fool thing will go away, then everyone will assume you've sent for help and ignore you. However, no man worth his salt will drive past delicate little you struggling bravely with one of those infernal machines called a car jack. I give you an absolute money-back guarantee that this will work.

And, if you have the bad luck to develop a flat on a road traveled only by females on their way to Women's Lib meetings, then it's handy to be able to go ahead and really fix the thing. *They* will assume you really *want* to do it yourself.

There is a marvelous invention called *instant air* that comes in a can about the size of a can of hair spray. I strongly recommend that you keep one in the trunk. You just insert its tube in the valve of your flat tire and press. It has enough air under pressure in it to inflate the tire and get you to the nearest service station—that is, if your flat was caused by a slow leak. Naturally, this stuff wouldn't work on a really sizeable puncture.

For this disaster, resign yourself to getting your hands dirty. In the trunk of your car should be a jack. It's important that you know how the jack works, and the *best* way is to watch someone who does know. Try to get your brother, husband, son, father, or that nice bachelor down the hall to give you a lesson. It's really not difficult.

Basically though, this is how it's done. The jack comes in two parts, a sturdy metal column that lifts and supports the car, and a long metal handle that acts as a pumping lever. You place the lifting surface, usually a broad plate at the top of the column, under a sturdy looking part of the undercarriage of the chassis near the flat. Insert the handle in a socket you'll find on the column of the jack and pump a few times until you feel it tighten against the car—but *not* until the wheel lifts off the ground. Take the jack handle and, using its flat end, pry off the chrome hubcap. Under it you'll find a series of nuts which hold the wheel on the car. Using the socket end of the jack handle now, loosen these nuts, a little at a time, going all the way around several times until you can move them with your fingers. But don't take them off yet.

Put the spare on the ground near the flat and put the chrome hubcap nearby, rounded side down. Put the handle back in and pump until the tire clears the ground by a few inches. Take the nuts off with your fingers, put them in the hubcap so they won't roll off into the landscape, and pull the wheel off the car.

Put the spare on the car and begin replacing those nuts. Again, you go all the way around, tightening a little with your fingers on each one.

Lower the car by pumping the jack handle until the tire is resting firmly on the ground. Using the socket end of the handle again, continue tightening the nuts until they seem firm and secure. Replace the hubcap, remove the jack, put it and the flat in the trunk, and head for the nearest service station. Get the attendant there to check the job you just did because the chances are you didn't get the nuts tight enough. It takes a pretty strong arm to do that. But, I'll bet you get some mighty admiring glances from the boys in the back, anyway. It isn't every woman who can change a tire!

STUCK HORN

There was a television commercial a while back where a fluttery little lady kept murmuring, "How embarrassing," to her friend's faux pas. You've probably felt the same way if your friend the Packard ever pulled the social error of getting its horn stuck in five o'clock traffic. You just sit there, cringing, while that mind-shattering din reverberates off every male motorist within half a mile, and the cop on the corner is ready to throttle you for making his thankless job even more trying.

If it ever happens to you again, just hitch up your girdle, stare 'em straight in their beady eyes, and go out and fix the darned thing! This is one of the easiest temporary repair jobs in the whole book.

Turn off the motor, lift the hood, and look for a snail-shaped contraption (the horn) up front near the radiator. Connected to it will be a wire with a plug that looks something like the wire on the back of your stereo. Simply disconnect this wire from the horn by pulling, gently, with your fingers. Magically, that infernal racket will cease and you can drive to the nearest service station and get the thing fixed.

WORN SHOCK ABSORBERS

Shock absorbers are just springs that help to make the ride a little smoother. If you suspect yours are going or a mechanic says you need them, here's a simple test to find out. Stand at one corner of your car and push down on the fender. As the fender comes up, push down again, and so on until the car is bounding merrily. Then, let go. The car should go up or down and then come to a stop in the middle. If it continues to bounce, you may need new shocks. You should test each corner because they operate independently.

THE BATTERY

The battery is a device for furnishing electrical power to your car. You should know a few basics about its care and feeding because when it quits, so does your car.

The next time you're at the service station and the attendant says he's going to check your battery, get out and watch what he does. He'll remove some little caps on the top of the battery and look inside, inspecting the level of the water there. It should be right up to the top. If it's not, he'll add *distilled* water. Now, you *can* do this yourself at home if you happen to have distilled water around. It's free at the station though. The level should be checked weekly, otherwise you're liable to find yourself with a sick battery on the very morning you're rushing to get to that fabulous new job.

You'll also see two cables attached to posts on the top of the battery. These carry the generated electricity from the battery to your car's electrical system (horn, ignition, lights, etc.). I hope you won't also see some icky looking gunk around those posts. If you do, don't worry, it's just corrosion that occurs in almost every battery once in a while; but it needs to be removed occasionally or all the battery's power may not get through.

To remove it, disconnect the cables by gripping them with your pliers and pulling up. Brush off the corrosion with a wire brush, smear some grease on the posts, and replace the cables with the pliers, pressing them down firmly. If you don't want to do this messy job yourself (and I don't blame you!), just remind your service station attendant that it needs doing.

One of these fine days you're liable to turn the key to the ignition, step on the accelerator, and absolutely nothing will happen. The problem could be any one of several things, but your battery is the most likely culprit.

Look at the battery cables to see if they are firmly attached. If they're not, you'll need to take those pliers and force them back on. If the cables are all right, then suspect a dead battery. Cold weather can cause this, or did you, by any chance, leave the lights burning? Even a parking light can drain a battery after a few hours.

For emergencies like this, it's a good idea to carry a set of jumper cables in the trunk of your car. These are a double set of long, rubber-covered wires with clamps on each end. You attach one set of clamps to the posts of your dead battery (carefully connecting negative wire to negative post, positive to positive), and one set to the posts of a car with a good battery. The working car starts its engine, you start yours—and your battery will pick up enough life from the good battery to turn your engine over. But, after your friend (the one who didn't let his battery die!) leaves, don't just throw the cables in the trunk and take off. In order to give the battery enough charge to get it started *again* in case you accidentally turn off the engine or it dies in traffic, you need to sit there with the motor running for ten minutes or so.

And, *never* put those jumper cables on the floor of your car. They pick up an acid from the batteries that will demolish your carpeting faster than a hoard of grasshoppers can go through a Kansas wheatfield. Always return them to the trunk.

Cold-Morning Starts (or Non-Starts!)

If you have trouble starting your car on cold mornings you might try the trick my red-headed friend in Missouri uses. As soon as she gets up on a frosty morning she grabs her electric heating pad and an old towel and stumbles out to the carport. She spreads the towel, then the heating pad, over the motor, plugs the cord into the garage outlet, turns the switch to "high," then goes back in to get herself pulled together for the day.

By the time she's ready to leave, the motor has warmed enough to turn over without trouble. Just be sure you use the towel to protect the fabric surface of the heating pad from all that grease and grime.

Another friend uses a different method to guarantee quick starts in the winter. Whenever the forecast is for way-below-freezing overnight lows, he plugs a trouble light into the garage electrical outlet and drapes it under the hood so it hangs freely near the motor. The warmth generated by the bulb is enough to keep the motor in workable condition and it only uses a few cents worth of electricity per night.

However, if you live as I do in a climate where below zero readings are common, you'll be wise to invest in a commercial engine heater. There are several types. The two most common, though, are the *block heater* and the *dip stick heater*.

A block heater costs around ten dollars and must be installed by the garage mechanic. The mechanic will probably charge you eight or ten dollars for installation. This heater is permanently attached to the motor. It has an electrical cord which you plug into the garage outlet for several hours or overnight. The electricity generated by the heater keeps the motor warm and it will turn right over no matter how cold the weather.

The dip stick heater costs about three dollars and requires no installation. It's just a metal rod on a handle which you put into the oil dip stick hole when the temperature is expected to hit bottom. There is an electrical cord attached to the handle which you plug into the garage outlet. The metal rod becomes quite hot and will keep the motor warm and toasty for quick starts. This is the kind I use. It's less expensive than a block heater and I can use it on the next car I buy, without more outlay of cash.

Replacing the Battery

If your battery doesn't go, then you don't go; so it pays to keep a check on this little black box under the hood. You'll know that the battery is about on its last leg when you have trouble starting on chilly days that aren't really cold enough for an engine heater to be used. If your service station attendant tells you the battery needs to be *recharged* (connected to an electrical device that puts the old get-up-and-go back into it), then you can figure its days are numbered. And, look for trouble if the battery has carried you through two full winters of cold weather starts.

The time to replace a battery is *before* you have to. They're all guaranteed for a specified number of months, but it doesn't pay to drive right up to the last day. You know how guarantees work. Fifteen minutes after the guarantee runs out, you'll stop dead in the middle of a Los Angeles freeway at 5:30 on a Friday afternoon. Since the patrolman won't let you stay there over the weekend while you shop for a new battery, you'll have to be towed away. This is the first expense. Then, when you get to the garage, the attendant will have a selection of batteries to sell you. The cheapest will be $89.95 plus your gold fillings. Since you can't move the car without a battery, and you don't have any way to go get one without your car, and you're just passing through anyway on your way to Lake Tahoe, you're stuck, lady, stuck.

The smart thing to do is sacrifice a couple of months on the guarantee and begin shopping for a good buy before you need it. Batteries come in many price ranges, and are guaranteed usually for from 18 months to 60 months, depending upon price and brand. You can figure the best buy by calculating the number of months in the guarantee against the price. For instance: let's say a battery guaranteed for 18 months costs $15.95. That comes out to 88 cents a month. The one next to it on the shelf carries a guarantee of 36 months and is priced at $24.95. That's about 69 cents a month. But, the fancy one whose manufacturer will stand behind it for 60 months costs $39. That's only 65 cents a month. So, on the basis of cost alone, the expensive one is the better buy.

However, other factors can enter into the decision. How long do you plan to keep the car? Only a year or two? Then, you'd be better off buying a battery with a 24 month guarantee.

Then there's the weather factor. If you live in Florida and the car is parked while you swim all the time, there isn't nearly as much strain on your battery as if you live in Billings, Montana. Cold weather does make a difference in the life of a battery.

Also, what have you loaded your jalopy down with? Power steering, power brakes, power windows, air conditioning, portable television, and a disappearing bar? Then, I wouldn't advise the cheapie battery. It just doesn't have enough reserve power to support you.

Another thing to consider is the trade-in offer. Some dealers will offer outrageous amounts for your old battery as a trade-in, then jack up the price of the new battery to compensate. Use your noodle and do a little arithmetic before you sign the check.

OVER-HEATED RADIATORS

The main purpose of the radiator is to hold water necessary to keep the engine cool. When that level gets too low, through leakage, evaporation, or whatever, you'll be warned by a red light flashing on your dashboard, a geyser of steam spewing out from under the hood, or both. Stop the car immediately, turn off the motor and raise the hood. Wad up a thick rag and very carefully *loosen* the radiator cap. *Do not try to remove it just yet!* It is hot and there is a lot of steam under pressure in that radiator. Just loosen it slightly and *jump back*. The steam will gradually escape beneath the loose cap. When all is clear, you can safely remove the cap and fill the radiator from a hose, can, or whatever is convenient. But, before you do, *turn the motor back on* and leave it running while you're pouring in the water—this is *very important* in order to keep the radiator from cracking wide open from the shock of cold water against hot metal.

To avoid overheating radiators, check the water level in the radiator occasionally when the engine is cold. It should come to within an inch or two of the top of the radiator. If it does not, pour in enough water to fill it. If the engine is cold, you don't have to have it running when you fill it.

ADDING THAT QUART OF OIL

Changing oil in the old buggy isn't hard, but it's pretty messy. Not many women want to tackle this job. But you can save a good bit of money between oil changes by putting in that quart or so necessary to keep your oil pressure up. You've seen the attendant pull out the dip stick, wipe it off, reinsert it, and then pull it out again to check for the oil level. If you're in good shape, the oil line will be on "full." If you're a quart low, the oil line will be at "add 1 quart." You can check this yourself.

There is a place on the side of your engine to pour in the oil. Its location varies from car to car, so get someone to point it out to you on your car. Get a little pouring spout from your discount store (it'll cost fifteen or twenty cents) and a quart of top quality oil. Push the spout into the oil can, put the spout down into the opening on the side of the engine, and simply let the oil drain in. That's all there is to it.

I pay 75 cents a quart for oil at my discount store. The same brand at my service station casts $1.35 a quart, including labor. So I figure I'm ahead 60 cents everytime I add a quart of oil myself. I usually reward myself for being so thrifty by spending the 60 cents on a hot fudge sundae! If you buy oil by the case, it's even cheaper.

Use a detergent oil marked "SE." As to oil weight, that depends in part on the place you live and the climate. Generally, for most parts of the U.S., you'll be able to use "10W-30" or "10W-40" oil. Don't let those numbers and letters frighten you. They're all clearly marked on the cans so you can't go wrong.

THE AIR FILTER

Another little item you can replace yourself is the air filter. This is a honeycomb-looking contraption that serves to filter dirt from the air before it gets into your engine, much as you vacuum cleaner bags do. It will be inside a big round container that looks like a huge doughnut, and you'll find it sitting right on top of the engine. Unscrew the wing-nut that holds the top of the doughnut, and lift that top off. The filter will be right there. It's not attached, so pick it up and remove the foam collar from its perimeter. Hold the filter up to the light. If it looks dirty and you can't see light through it, you need another one.

Filters come in different sizes but don't haul that dirty old one down to the store for matching. The store will have a list of sizes posted. Just tell the salesman the make and model of your car and he'll get the right one for you.

Back home, throw away the old filter and wash out that foam collar in some kind of solvent. Put the collar on the new

Fig. 13-1. If carrying gasoline in your car trunk, stand it in a concrete block so it can't spill.

filter, place it back in the doughnut and you've increased your gasoline mileage, added life to the old buggy, and saved some money in the bargain. This needs to be done regularly—several times a year, probably—depending upon the amount you drive.

OUT OF GAS!

It's a good idea for a woman driving alone to carry a small, *tightly* closed one-gallon can of gasoline in the trunk—it's just good insurance against being stranded. This used to bother me. I was always afraid the can would tip over and start leaking. Then a friend showed me a clever trick and my worrying days (about this) are over. All you have to do is get a plain old concrete building block and set it in the trunk. Fit the gasoline can inside one of the block's holes, and there is no *way* the can can spill (Fig. 13-1).

Now, if you run your car *completely* dry before stopping to add that extra gallon, you may find the car still refusing to start. In that case, you'll need to prime the carburetor. Don't panic. This isn't any harder than priming a balky backyard water pump (of course *we* aren't old enough to remember the backyard water pump but we've seen them in the movies, right?)

Remember that air filter? Well, go back and look at it again. In the middle of the air filter's center hole you'll find the carburetor. It's just an open-topped metal box with a hinged flap in it. Its purpose is to mix air with gasoline for proper combustion. It's possible to run your car so dry of gasoline that there is none left in the carburetor. This is when you prime it. Just tilt that gasoline can up again and allow a spoonful or two (there is always that much left because you can't empty it completely into your tank) to drain into the carburetor. It should start then without trouble.

CLEAN IS BEAUTIFUL!

That lovely shiny finish on your car will last a long, long time with minimum care. And, according to the automobile manufacturers, regular washing and waxing can mean several hundred dollars more at trade-in time.

Most cars today come with a factory waxed finish that won't need replacing for many months, perhaps a year. All that's necessary to preserve the gleam is to keep the dirt and road grime cleaned away.

A weekly washing will do it. Have you tried one of those coin-operated car washes? I think they're the greatest thing since sliced bread. They're fast, cheap, and thorough. You can buzz your car in, covered with dust after a long Saturday of country auctions, spend a quarter or two and drive out five minutes later, squeaky clean and beautiful.

If you'd rather do it yourself, fine—but do it right. A botched wash job can permanently damage the finish.

According to the American Automobile Club, the important thing is to keep the car wet the entire time you're working on it. Begin with a thorough hosing down to remove dust and leave the water running until you're finished. That way, loosened grime and suds are carried away before they can dry and adhere to the finish.

If your car is only slightly dirty, just plain clear water may do the trick. For a heavy accumulation of grime, use a commercial car cleaner or your mild dish detergent, *never* a laundry or heavy-duty detergent.

Start at the top and, using a soft, lint-free cloth such as an old tee shirt, soap down an area as large as your arm can reach at a time. Then, flush away the dirty suds with running water immediately before you go on to another area. Finish off by scrubbing the tires and wheels. A little rubbing with your kitchen steel wool soap pad will make the white walls snowy again.

Bird droppings, bugs, and road tar can survive even the most conscientious wash job. Very gentle rubbing with a pad of nylon net dipped in water will take care of the first two offenders on paint, radiator grill, headlights, or windshield. Never, never use steel wool on paint! You could find yourself looking at a spot of bare metal within seconds.

Kerosene or turpentine will dissolve any road tar you might pick up. Do not use lacquer thinner—it can remove the paint, too! After the car is clean, dry it to prevent streaks. You can use that tee shirt, wrung out, for this. Or, for a really elegant effect, try a chamois. They're extremely absorbent and they completely eliminate streaking and water spotting. Don't throw that chamois down on the driveway when you're finished, though. Grease and grime are no-no's for a delicate chamois. Just rinse it out thoroughly, wring, and dry before putting away.

You can treat the inside of the car much as you would the same materials in your home. Vacuum the carpet thoroughly and shampoo with your usual rug shampoo if it needs it. Clean vinyl upholstery with your regular heavy-duty household cleaner. If you're lucky enough to have leather upholstery, give it the deluxe treatment with regular shampooing topped off with a specially formulated leather conditioner. This will keep it soft and gleaming for many years.

Wipe the dashboard, steering wheel, and interior chrome trim with a damp cloth or chamois. Don't use any abrasives here—you could easily scratch the finishes.

Simply clean the windows as you do the windows in your home, with a standard window cleaner or ammonia. Never use any oily solvent such as kerosene on automobile glass, even to remove bugs. It will leave a film that is exceedingly difficult to remove and it can cause the dangerous "halo" effect that distorts vision at night.

There are commercial cleaners made to remove small rust spots from chrome bumpers and trim but a hard typewriter eraser will do just as well. They have a slightly gritty ingredient which does the job very nicely without scratching. Or, crumple up a piece of aluminum foil into a ball and rub the spot briskly.

Did you know that it's just as important to keep the underside of your car clean as it is the pretty part that shows? Road salts are deposited under the chassis as you drive and, little by little, they corrode the metal until big, ugly, expensive-to-repair holes appear. This is especially true if you live near the ocean or where road crews sand and salt highways in the winter. It's a good practice to squirt plenty of water under the car when you wash it, paying special attention to the fenders and the edges of the body. Or, use a super idea I heard not long ago. Just set your revolving lawn sprinkler under the car and turn the water on full force!

There is a professional protective undercoating applied by garages which will give your car protection from corrosion. It costs about $80 and will last and last. In the long run, it can be a very good investment.

About twice a year you'll need to follow the weekly washing with a waxing. Unless the finish is in really bad condition, one of the combination cleaner-wax formulas will do it. They come in pressurized cans and are a breeze to apply. Just spray on a small area at a time and wipe dry, no harder to use than your spray furniture polish. Work in the shade or in a garage if possible to prevent the polish from running from the hot sun or hardening too quickly from the cold.

Sometimes the paint on an older car will become so dull through oxidation that this cleaner-wax combination won't do the job. You need a professional cleaning and waxing then. Your service station will use a slightly abrasive liquid specially made to remove accumulated dead paint and dirt too stubborn to wash off. Then follow with a paste wax to bring back the shine.

BUYING A CAR

In the first place, when buying a car, stop and ask youself, "Do I really need this car?" They are expensive little toys and often don't warrant the expense involved. Aside from the original cost, did you know that it will cost you from $1100 to $1500 per year just to own it? This includes plates, insurance, and depreciation, plus the tires, gas, oil, tune-ups and repairs necessary just to keep it running. If you live in a metropolitan area, think how many bus and taxi rides you could have for that.

I'll grant you, though, that in many parts of this country your own wheels are the only way to get around. In that case, it pays you to get the most for your money when you do buy the little cream puff.

If, like most of us, such terms as *torque* and *overhead cams* sound like a foreign language to you, then rely on the advice of a knowledgeable friend when it comes to shopping for that new car. Aside from knowing where to kick the tires, many men do understand the mysteries that go on underneath the hood. One friendly word of advice, though. Be very skeptical of the advice you get from teenaged boys. Admittedly, they probably know more about the mechanics of an auto than Henry Ford himself. But they also tend to think that any engine with less than 545 horsepower is fit only for a lawnmower. Leave the little dears to their fast get-a-way numbers. We don't need them. I'm driving a low horsepower International Scout II now, and although it would never qualify for the Indianapolis 500, it gets me to work every day and over the roughest roads in the west on the weekends. So, rely on the advice of a good friend who has had several cars—and rely on your own good judgment when you go wandering through those glittering showrooms.

Buying a new car is a little like going to an auction. If you don't decide before you get there just how much you can spend you're liable to end up with a very expensive white elephant and bankruptcy notices. Write the figure you decide upon down on a piece of paper and wrap it around your pen—the one you'll sign that purchase agreement with.

If you live in a hot climate, air conditioning is not a luxury. Neither are power steering and power brakes if you can afford the initial cost. When you go to trade the car in you'll get the money back. But automatic windows, racing stripes, tachometers, and yards and yards of chrome may not pay for themselves at trade-in time. So don't let all these glamorous extras add hundreds of dollars to the last line of your contract.

And when it comes time to arranging financing, shop around just as much as you did when the office dreamboat invited you to an afternoon at the races and you didn't have a thing to wear. The rates you'd have to pay the automobile dealer to carry your contract may be much higher than what you'd get at a bank.

Granted, there is nothing like a new car. But often the simple balance in our bank accounts dictates buying a used car. And, if you shop well, used cars can be just as good a buy and just as satisfying as next year's model. Some people even prefer to buy a top-of-the-line used car because the "bugs" have usually been worked out of it by the previous owner.

A few rules of thumb to consider when buying a used car are:

1. Learn the market. Check the prices in the Sunday paper. Ask at your service station. See what the latest *Consumer's Report* says about the reliability and repair history of various makes.
2. Examine each possibility realistically. A car which needs $100 worth of new tires to put it in top shape would be a better buy than one with great tires and an exhaust that pours out a cloud of blue smoke. That means expensive oil burning and maybe the need for a ring job.
3. Buy from someone you can trust. Lots which sell only used cars and are not affiliated with a new car dealer may be suspect. Sometimes they buy the cars which a new car dealer takes in trade and doesn't feel are good enough to carry his warranty. Even more potentially dangerous are cars advertised by individuals in the daily papers. You have absolutely no guarantee or knowledge of how that car was treated. If it collapses ten minutes after you buy it, you're just out of luck. Your safest bet is the used car lot of a reputable new car dealer. Chances are the car you buy from him has been reconditioned in his garage by his well-trained mechanics, and put in good condition.
4. Buy when new cars are selling well. That's when the used car lots will be full and the dealers will be anxious to move their stock. This is usually spring and summer.
5. Know values. As a rule, a car two to four years old is your best buy. If you find a virtually new car at a rock-bottom price, ask yourself "Why?" Could be it's a lemon, always was a lemon, and always will be a lemon. Maybe the previous owner just got rid of it in

desperation. Don't be hesitant about asking the name and phone number of a former owner so you can make some inquiries of your own. If the car is a genuine value, the dealer will be glad to give this information to you.

6. Don't let new carpeting, new seat covers, or a shiny coat of paint tempt you. These are inexpensive flourishes some dealers use to blind you to a car's faults.

7. Finally, if your town has a diagnostic center, take the car to it before you sign on the dotted line. For a reasonable fee, the center will give you an honest evaluation of the car's worth. Lacking a diagnostic center, go to a service station you trust for the same report.

THINGS TO CHECK REGULARLY

Cars, like children, thrive on regularity, and the proper care will save you many trips to the shop and much hard-earned money. I suggest you type out a card containing the following information and glue it inside your glove compartment:

1. Recommended tire pressure
2. Oil weight
3. Tire size
4. The dates to have regular checkups (probably twice a year) on brakes, lights, gasoline filter, anti-freeze, etc.
5. Dates for lubrication and oil changes. (This is determined by the car you drive and will be listed in your manual.)

Although only a regular checkup by your friendly neighborhood mechanic will spot many potential troublemakers before they hatch, there are some basic symptoms you should watch for yourself.

A decided "knocking" when you step on the gas pedal, or a general sluggishness, could mean you need a tune-up.

Listen when your car is shifting its gears. If you hear any abnormal noises, have the transmission checked *immediately*. You could save yourself a bill of several hundred dollars.

Is the steering wheel hard to turn? Does it vibrate? Does the car wander all over the road? Have the steering mechanism checked and also the wheel alignment.

The brake pedal should *never* touch the floor on regular brakes. If it begins pressing to within two inches of the floor, have the brakes checked. Power brakes shouldn't depress much more than three-fourths of an inch.

Naturally, any unusual whine, screech, roar, or bump means you should stop immediately and have the car examined. Many times a minor repair when you first notice a noise can save real major repairs later after the wheel bearings have worn out or the brake linings have died.

Never, never discount your natural feminine ingenuity! My car once stopped dead at 6:45 a.m. at the intersection of two minor highways. A quick examination showed me the problem was with the battery cables. Now, if I had had some tools along I would have been on my way in three minutes. I didn't have any, though. The only tool in the car was a Coors beer can opener. Well, I'd admit it took a bit of doing—and more than one early morning commuter did a doubletake at the tousled strawberry blond draped over the fender of the trusty green convertible at that hour of the morning—but within fifteen minutes that beer can opener and I had the car running again. It sure beat walking for help.

So, really *look* under the hood of your car. Get to know what makes it tick. Ask questions, and above all, don't be afraid to try!

14

The Great Outdoors

And How to Keep Your

Share of it from Falling Apart

All you ladies who inhabit high rise apartments or luxury condominiums can skip this chapter because it's filled with nuggets of wisdom on keeping the *outside* of the home attractive and in reasonable repair.

There really is very little difference in the maintenance of the outside and the inside of your home as far as effort is concerned. I just happen to like working outside more.

Besides, if you work outside, the whole neighborhood can see the results of your cleverness and energy—gutters that actually drain water, cute little stepping stones all over the place, a smooth, weed-free driveway! There's nothing quite so good for the ego of a feminine do-it-yourselfer as an admiring, "Say, that really looks great!" from the ancient and venerable fraternity of Saturday morning fence leaners. Your husband will beam. Or, if you're single, one of the fence leaners might just mention to the new fellow at work on Monday morning, "You know, there's this clever little girl in our neighborhood. You really ought to meet her..."

But, back to business. Let's tackle that driveway first.

WEEDS IN THE DRIVEWAY

Is anything as persistent as a weed? We spend half our lives fertilizing, pruning, mulching, and singing to the rhododendron, and what does it do? Turns yellow and shrivels to dust the minute we sneak off for a weekend. But a weed? You can lay four inches of blacktop over it, drive on it for a year, expose it to sub-zero temperatures in the winter and a dry summer that would make the Great Dust Bowl look like a rain forest, and it will push through a crack the next summer healthier than ever and with a brace of relatives to boot.

But you're smarter than any weed, so outwit the dastardly pests! First you kill the weed. Get a weed killer from the hardware store or garden shop. The driveway is one area where you can go all out with a humdinger weed killer that will really zap those weeds since you don't have to worry about it seeping into nearby flowerbeds. Pour in the recommended dosage wherever a wily weed has pushed its way through the blacktop.

Now, get a can of blacktop sealer from the hardware or building supply store. With a trowel, poke the sealer into all those cracks, filling them well up to the top. The sealer will form a bond with the original blacktop, making a good tight seal.

There's no long wait for the sealer to dry or set. You can drive on it within a couple of hours. But, watch out about getting in on your shoes. It *will* stick to them a bit at first, and you don't want a blacktopped carpet, too!

Now, get back to singing to the rhododendron. With luck, you've put an end to the weeds.

CLOGGED DOWNSPOUTS ON GUTTERS

You can keep the downspouts on your gutters from clogging up with leaves by placing a screen across the opening of the downspout. Building supply houses carry an easy-to-install type that looks something like a miniature wire birdcage. You slip it into the opening at the upper edge of the downspout where it acts as a sieve, allowing water to drain through but stopping the leaves and debris.

If your local store doesn't carry these gadgets, you can contrive a sieve yourself. Cut a circle of large-meshed wire—such as chicken wire or hardware cloth—large enough to cover the hole in the downspout. Put two or three dollops of liquid metal cement at the edges to secure it. This is just about as effective as the commercial sieve.

True, you'll get an accumulation of leaves in the gutter itself and they'll have to be removed occasionally. But it is much easier to get up there and sweep leaves from the gutter than to try to free a jammed downspout.

LEAKING GUTTERS

A leaking gutter is little better than none at all. If it's really *leaking*, now, not overflowing from an accumulation of debris, you'll need a bit of roofing tar to seal the seams together again. This is the same stuff used to patch holes in roofs, seal flashing around chimneys, etc. It's a thick, icky gunk that is the dickens to handle, but it does the job. You can buy a small can at the hardware store for less than half a dollar.

Frankly, I wouldn't mess up a good brush applying the stuff because, believe me, even the thriftiest of you wouldn't try to clean or salvage that brush. A small stick or one of those wooden paint paddles (free from the paint store) will do fine.

Get a glob of tar on the end of the stick or paddle and swipe it all over the seams on the *inside* of the gutter. Be sure to seal the end caps as well as the connectors between the long pieces of guttering. It isn't necessary to put the tar anywhere except at the seams. This won't be the neatest repair job you ever do, but no one will see it except the squirrels. And, as long as it stops those leaks, who cares?

STEPPING STONES

Stepping stones add charm to almost any garden, and you can make your own for a fraction of the cost of ready-mades. You can use forms—shallow wooden frames hinged on the sides—to shape the stones, but this is pretty slow going. And no sensible woman wants to spend all her free time messing around with concrete when she really should be practicing her tennis swing!

Besides having to build the frame for a form, you must wait a day after pouring the concrete *in* before you can take the hardened blocks *out*. If you build three forms you can only make three blocks a day, obviously. So, either you make a *lot* of forms, or you take forever to get enough stones to go from the side door to the hammock. And by that time, summer will be over and you won't want to get to the hammock, anyway.

It's much simpler to form the stepping stones right in the ground where they are to stay. It's not quite so professional, I'll admit, but it's faster, cheaper, and easier.

The ground should be slightly damp for best results, not sopping wet or bone dry. Mow the grass down as low as you can without damaging it.

Then take a few minutes to decide a graceful path for the walk, and just how far apart you want the stones. Is anything more annoying than to have to leap like a gazelle from one step to another simply because the walk was laid out by a 6′8″ man who set the walk to fit *his* long legs? So take your own natural stride into consideration when you space the holes. Now, cut the design you want into the soil—round stones, square stones, or free-form stones—with a sharp shovel. Make the cuts about three inches deep with smooth, vertical sides. Cut as many holes as stepping stones you'll want, and cut them exactly where they are to stay.

Hie yourself on down to your friendly building supply dealer who carries a dry concrete mix in large bags. There are different types of mix for different jobs, so be sure you tell him you are making stepping stones. As a rule of thumb, figure about one bag of concrete mix for each three stepping stones (one foot square) you plan to make.

Before you go any farther into this project you'll need to go into the house and collect a few wire coat hangers. Surprised? Well, all concrete should be reinforced against cracking, and coat hangers are ideal for small jobs. If you have wire cutters or pliers with a wire-cutting edge, cut each coat hanger into two or three pieces. Lacking the wire-cutters, just bend the coat hangers in half, flatten and wire them together so they won't spring apart.

Now back to the job...

There are good directions on the bag for mixing the concrete, but, briefly, you pour the mix, one bag at a time, into a wheelbarrow and add water, mixing with a hoe, until it is about the consistency of very thick mud (Fig. 14-1). You'll probably feel just like a little girl again, mixing up a batch of mud pies on a lazy July afternoon! But, you're a big girl now, with your beauty to think about, so wear sturdy rubber gloves. The lime in that cement is murder on the hands.

When you're satisfied there are no dry patches left in the mix, begin pouring it into the holes. Pour each one about one-half full. Now, reach down to your pile of cut-up coat hangers and pick up a few pieces. Lay them on top of the concrete you've poured, then go ahead and finish pouring until the holes are full. If you can get them to mound up just a bit in the center, so much the better.

Take a short piece of board and jiggle it across the wet concrete to settle and flatten it.

You're going to take a short break now (how short depends upon the temperature), while waiting for the concrete to *set up* (that means stiffen).

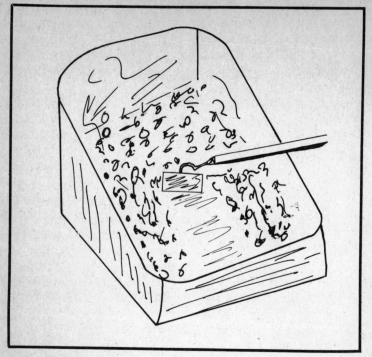

Fig. 14-1. Mix concrete in a wheelbarrow until it is the consistency of very thick mud.

If you think you've gotten the hang of mixing concrete, you can use this time to mix another batch and pour three more stones. Don't do it, though, if you feel it will take you more than thirty minutes or so.

In approximately a half hour, go back to the first three stones you poured. By then, the concrete should be getting fairly firm. Take another short board and smooth the surface of the concrete again, using a slow, circular motion.

Those three are finished now and you can go on back to the second batch.

Come tomorrow you'll have a lovely set of stepping stones to admire. Don't expect these to be as smooth and sterile looking as those you could buy in the garden supply shop. There's just no way. These will have *character*—a bump here, a wrinkle there. But, they'll serve the purpose you made them for and you did make them *yourself!* That means a lot.

Just a couple of words of caution, though, from experience. Plan to make these stepping stones at a time when you aren't likely to be interrupted. Once that concrete is mixed, it will go ahead and set up on schedule, believe me. Just because you had a once-in-a-lifetime invitation to ride the roller coaster at Coney Island won't make a bit of difference to the stuff. Leave it and you'll come back to find a wheelbarrow full of rock-hard concrete.

Also, plan for a dry day with an absolutely zero chance of rain. I once spent a whole afternoon laying steps from a back door to the back gate, and had them perfectly smooth and level. (Well, to be honest, they were passably smooth and level.) I went inside and was just pouring the bubble bath into the tub when I heard the patter of little raindrops on the roof. Within minutes it was raining buckets. Next morning I found my stones, all nice and hard, with miserable little pock marks all over them. Very discouraging.

LEAKY GARDEN HOSE

It doesn't do much good to try to water the marigolds with a hose that has a dozen little geysers between the nozzle and the faucet. All you'll do is sprinkle the cat, who won't appreciate it one bit.

So, fix that leaky hose. Sometimes a very small leak can be repaired by simply wrapping it tightly with electrician's tape. But, the best and most permanent repair is done by cutting the damaged part completely out of the hose and then joining the cut edges with a metal splicer.

You get this splicer at—where else?—the hardware store. It is a strange contraption that looks something like a mad artist's metal sculpture of two shriveling daisies joined together back to back. There are little tubes inside each daisy's "petals" which you push into the two cut ends of the hose. By compressing the petals very tightly into the hose with a wrench or pliers, you make a good solid watertight connection. It's really very easy to do. Just be sure to buy the right *size* splicer. It should be the same diameter as the hose.

SCATTERED GARBAGE

Of course, you could take it as a compliment to your cooking that the neighborhood dogs would rather forage in your garbage can than in that of the lady next door who graduated magna cum laude from Cordon Bleu. It's possible that you're a better cook than she, but it's a lot more probable that she also learned how to keep the scavengers out of her garbage can.

If you're tired of cleaning up around the garbage can every morning, try this simple little device to keep the lid securely locked onto the can. Get a firm screen-door spring at the hardware store. You'll find it is just the right size to fit across your garbage can lid. Now take a wire coat hanger and cut two pieces from it, each about eight inches or so long. With your pliers, bend these pieces of wire so they look like giant fish hooks. Slip the long, uncurved end of one piece of wire through the ring at one end of the spring and bend it back on itself so it is firmly attached and can't be pulled off. Do the same thing to the other end of the spring with the other "hook." You now have a screen door spring with a big hook attached to each end.

That's all the work involved. Pass the spring through the handle on top of the lid and slip the fish hooks under the handles on each side of the can (Fig. 14-2). It'll be tight enough that the dogs can't nose it off, but easy for you to remove to dump in another sack of chicken bones. If your garbage pick-up men are the type who would probably fling the spring into their truck along with the bone, just bend one of the hooks around its handle, permanently. You, and the garbage men, can still remove the other end to get into the can.

BROWN STREAKS ON OUTSIDE WALLS

If you notice ugly brown streaks running down your home's exterior siding, it is probably from nails which have rusted and are bleeding through the paint. To correct it you'll need to first sand away the paint over each nail until the head is exposed. Coat each nail with shellac then countersink the nail with your nail set about a quarter of an inch or so into the siding. Fill the resulting holes with putty. After the putty has dried thoroughly, repaint the holes and the brown streaks.

DAMP FLOOR ON PORCH OR BREEZEWAY

In some climates a concrete porch or breezeway floor will become absolutely wet in damp weather. There isn't anything you can do to the floor to stop this. It's just moisture percolating up through the soil and the concrete, and is the result of a poor foundation. You can put a decking on *top* of the concrete, though, which will be dry and comfortable no matter how drippy the weather.

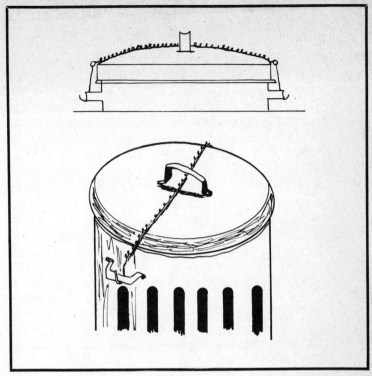

Fig. 14-2. Use a screen door spring to secure a garbage can lid.

Some lumber dealers carry ready-made sections of redwood decking. They come in set sizes— 3′ × 4′, 3′ × 3′, etc. You merely buy the number and sizes to cover your porch floor (if it happens to be of a size that will accommodate those ready-made sections) and put them down. No installation is necessary.

However, it will be less expensive, and you'll get a custom deck that extends from wall to wall, if you build it yourself. The most practical way to go is to use redwood 2 × 4s throughout. Redwood is more costly than pine, but it is virtually rot-proof and is attractive and durable without any painting, staining, or varnishing. So you save the cost of a finish coat, plus the trouble of putting it on.

You're going to put a series of these 2 × 4 boards on edge (that is, the two-inch side against the floor), every two feet, to serve as supports. You'll lay other boards on top of these supports at right angles, with a quarter-inch of space between them. Nail the top boards to the support boards with 4 1/2 inch galvanized nails. Don't try to lay out a whole floor at once. Put all the support boards in place, then nail on the top boards one at a time.

Measure your floor carefully to avoid waste and piecing. For instance, if the floor is eight feet wide and twelve feet long you'll need seven boards eight feet long for the supports (one for each end and five in between) and 24 boards twelve feet long (they're four inches wide, therefore three to the foot) for the top decking. Draw a plan of your floor to scale on paper before you order the lumber.

DETERIORATING CONCRETE

Those de-icing chemicals and salts we use in the winter melt that slippery ice all right, but they play havoc with the surface of the driveway and sidewalk. It's far better to shovel the snow away before it turns to ice, and to use sand on the icy spots that do form.

However, you can't stop the road salts that drip off the car onto your driveway. So, you should know how to protect that expensive concrete from deterioration. The best, and least expensive, treatment is a simple coating of boiled linseed oil and kerosene. Mix them half and half, and use about one gallon per 40 square yards on concrete. Don't apply the mixture to wet concrete. It should dry a day or two after a rain or hosing before the treatment. Apply one coat, wait a few hours for it to be absorbed, then apply a second coat.

If the protection is to be applied to concrete which has already been exposed to de-icing salts, you'll need to brush away all scaled concrete then scrub the driveway and flush with clear water to remove as much of the imbedded salt as possible. Allow the concrete to dry for a day before coating it with the linseed oil/kerosene mixture.

Caution The concrete will very likely be sticky or slippery for several days following this treatment so *watch your step*.

CRACKS AND CREVICES

What weatherstripping does for your doors and windows, caulking will do for crevices around those door and window *frames*, for cracks in stucco, for the openings around pipes as they enter your home, and for making an air-tight seal around window air conditioners. Caulking is one of the best ways to seal your home against unwanted air and moisture.

You know how miserably uncomfortable a drafty house can be in winter. Well, a good caulking job can stop many of those air leaks, and you'll be amazed at the difference in comfort and fuel savings.

And don't ever think those tiny cracks in your stucco walls aren't serious. They are, and they can cause damage amounting to many hundreds of dollars if left untreated. Water can seep in, eventually causing the wood frame of the house to rot. In cold climates, even small amounts of moisture in those cracks will freeze, enlarging them until, finally, big ugly chunks of stucco fall away from the wall. It will pay you to inspect those exterior walls frequently and caulk whenever you find the beginning of a crack.

There are many different types of caulking which we'll go into in a minute, but they are basically all sealing compounds used to stop leakage of some sort.

When you go to the store to buy that caulking you may be confronted with a confusing number of technical-sounding names. As always, rely upon your friend, the dealer, to recommend the best one for *your* job. A brief course in caulking terminology won't hurt, though, so here goes:

Caulking Gun—a simple device used to apply some sealants, consisting of a metal housing with a trigger at the end. The caulk itself is packaged in a cartridge which looks much like a tube of toothpaste. You cut the nozzle of the cartridge at an angle, then puncture the inner seal with a nail to release the caulking. The cartridge is then inserted into the caulking gun. By pressing the trigger, you can guide a line of the caulk into cracks that need filling. To stop the flow of caulk, you disengage the rod of the gun and pull it back. Seal the end of the nozzle with a tight cap of masking tape before you store it. Then the next time you find a crack that needs attention, the caulk will be soft and the gun ready for action.

Rope-Form Caulk—one of the easiest forms of caulk for the lady do-it-yourselfer to use. It comes coiled in ropes and you just pull off a strand or two (according to the size of the crack) and press it into place. Rope caulk is not a permanent seal and shouldn't be used where there are cracks in stucco or where one section of a wall joins another. It *is* useful to fill in around air conditioners, or for a temporary seal around windows. It cannot be painted satisfactorily, however.

Oil-Based Caulks—low in cost, usually sold in cartridges and applied with a caulking gun. This type should be used only on joints where little or no expansion is likely to occur. It should be painted to prolong its lifespan. Wait for the caulk to set and cure, though, before you paint. The instructions on the cartridge will tell how long.

Flexible Sealants—useful for joints where some degree of flexibility is required. They may be used in cracks where both sides of the crack are of the same material and may also be used as a glazing material when putting new glass into window frames. The flexible sealants shrink up to 35 percent of their mass, and therefore should not be used on deep cracks.

Water-Based Acrylic Latex Caulks—easy to apply and don't require much preparation. You can apply these to a damp surface, smooth them out with water and a putty knife, and paint almost immediately. These sealants adhere to almost any surface and remain flexible.

Solvent-Based Acrylics—do not require primers, adhere to almost any surface and have a very long life expectancy. They have a strong odor, however, and should not be used in enclosed areas where food is stored or prepared.

Elastomeric Sealants—excellent for us weekend repair ladies. They can be used on almost any crack or joint, they adhere well to any surface, they require no primer and they form a durable rubber-like seal which will last up to 20 years. They are a little more expensive than other sealants, however.

Read the label carefully regardless of which type of caulk you choose to use. As a general rule of thumb, you should clean out the crack first. Chip out any old dried caulk and brush it with a stiff-bristled brush. If the caulk requires a primer, use the correct one.

Sealant can't get into a crack that is too small, so you may need to enlarge yours up to a quarter-inch or more. On the other hand, a crack that is *too* large (well over a half-inch in size) will probably need some back-up filling before you caulk. Don't use oakum. Your dealer will probably recommend a non-staining rubber or polyethylene filler.

One last work of advice. Think ahead. It's much more pleasant to deepen your suntan while you caulk in the good old summertime—when you don't *need* to seal out the cold wind—than six months later when there's a foot of snow on the ground and the chill factor in your living room is 90 below. Most caulks won't work below 40 degrees anyway. They get too stiff to flow smoothly.

15

Lagniappe

A Little Something Extra

There's a delightful old custom in southern Louisiana which is one of the reasons many people go to New Orleans to visit, fall in love with its gentle hospitality, and never leave. It's the giving of *lagniappe*. Lagniappe means "a little something extra" and is always the gift of the heart. It means 13 sugar cookies for a tiny charmer instead of the dozen she paid for. It's an extra bus stop in the middle of the block so an elderly gentleman won't have to walk so far to his front door. It's the bottle of champagne delivered to a bridal suite by an incurably romantic hotel proprietor.

This chapter is a lagniappe for you—bits of unrelated information that I hope will make your life easier and more enjoyable.

Disguising An Unpleasant View

Need light but hate the sight of that messy apartment service yard? Get four wood slats from the lumber company and cut them to fit the inside of that window frame. Nail them in place, forming an inner frame inside the old one. Cut a sheet of filigree-patterned hardboard or decorative plastic to fit this new frame and glue in place (Fig. 15-1). Lovely! You won't be able to open the window, of course, but I'll bet you never did anyway.

Fig. 15-1. Disguising an unpleasant view.

Frames That Mar Walls

You can stop the lower edges of heavy picture or mirror frames from marking the walls by pushing a rubber-headed nail (from the plumbing section of the hardware store) into each lower corner.

Sanding Small Items

It's easy to sand small items if you'll tack sandpaper to a flat surface and rub the material over *it* rather than try to rub the sandpaper over the tiny item.

Fixing Chipped Glassware

Found a chip in the lip of your favorite cut glass pitcher? Or a rough edge on your glass-topped coffee table? Try this trick that I've seen antique dealers use to salvage damaged glass. Wrap fine garnet paper around a sponge or piece of foam rubber and rub the rough edge gently and persistently. Massage a bit of mineral oil on for a finishing touch after the glass is smooth again.

Anchoring Tiny Hinges

Those tiny decorative hinges on jewelry and trinket boxes often work loose. To avoid completely resetting them, just brush a coat of plain shellac over each side of the hinge, wait a few minutes for it to become tacky, push the nails back in, and press the hinge firmly in place (Fig. 15-2).

Using Shellac as Glue

The same shellac can be used to glue several difficult materials together. Try it for glass to glass, leather to metal or leather to wood. Spread a coat of the shellac thickly on each surface, wait for it to become tacky, then press together.

"Walking" Cutting Board

Portable cutting boards are handy but too often they tend to jump all over the cabinet as you pound away at the Swiss steak. To remedy this, by a package of rubber-headed nails at the hardware store. These are just half rounds of hard rubber on a small spike. Hammer one into each corner of the board and you shouldn't have any more trouble. I found after doing this that it not only stopped the bouncing around, but really improved the appearance of the board, and, as a bonus, made the board easier to pick up.

Fixing Damaged Formica

There is always one section of the kitchen Formica which receives more wear than the rest. As a result, it becomes scarred and ugly long before the rest is ready for replacement. Spruce up this damaged section by gluing a wooden cutting board onto the cabinet top with epoxy glue. You'll have an attractive working surface for years to come.

Devising Temporary Eye Protection

Your ski or skin-diving goggles make excellent temporary eye protectorc when you're cutting glass or working around any dangerous flying debris.

Stuck Tight?

It's extremely frustrating to see that glue or shellac in the jar but not be able to get to it because the lid is stuck tight.

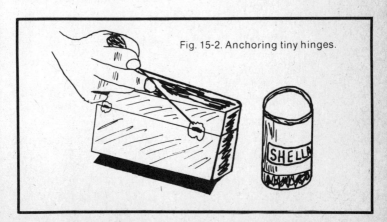

Fig. 15-2. Anchoring tiny hinges.

Eliminate this traumatic experience by coating the inside of the cap, the threaded part, generously with petroleum jelly the first time it's open. Use this trick on any liquid that tends to make a permanent bond (your nail polish?) with its bottle. You'll need to renew the petroleum jelly occasionally.

Determining Auction Values

Are you an auction hound, too? Then you know how easy it is to get carried away and bid more than that garden tractor (with attachments) is really worth. Next time, take a Montgomery Ward or Sears catalog along to use as a price reference. Then, you'll know if $200 is really a bargain.

Measuring Several Lengths of Wood

If you're cutting several pieces of wood the same length, don't use one to measure the next. You'll tend to make each one just a fraction of an inch longer than the one before. Use one measuring guide for all.

Removing Decals

Did your child drop out of Podunk U. and insist that the decal be removed from the car immediately? Or have you lost your affection for the man from ZZZ fraternity and suddenly discovered one from XXX, and you have to get that ZZZ decal off your motorcycle windshield before this afternoon at the very latest? Relax. Just get out your portable steamer (the one you use to de-wrinkle your orange wool gaberdine) and fire away at the offending symbols. They should peel right off.

Devising Disposable Brushes

Use one of your cotton-tipped swabs when you need a tiny paint brush or glue applicator. They're cheap, handy, and disposable.

Identifying Storm Windows

Replacing storm windows or screens on various sized windows after storage won't be such a guessing game if you'll mark each with an identifying number as you take it down.

Storing the Ironing Board

Think there's no place to store your ironing board, and you're sick to death of stumbling over it? Cheer up! Save the next two large size thread spools you empty, get two long

Fig. 15-3. Storing the ironing board.

screws to fit through the center holes and open the nearest closet door. Drill two pilot holes in the door, slip the screws through the spools, and insert them into the door. Now, hang up the ironing board and smile again (Fig. 15-3).

Protecting Seldom-Used Locks From Corrosion

Moisture, sand, and dirt can have a devastating effect on those outdoor locks which are seldom operated. In time, the locks may become completely corroded and unusable. To protect them, place a piece of adhesive or electricians tape over the keyhole. This will be easy to remove and replace when you need to open the lock.

Improvising a Clamp

Many glued objects must be clamped tightly in order to guarantee a secure bond. Not many of us keep a supply of clamps around but you can rig up an excellent one in a couple of minutes.

Remember your First Aid training in Girl Scouts? You can still make a tourniquet, can't you? That's what you're going to do. Just cut a length of cord and tie it loosely around the glued object. Insert a stick underneath the cord and twist it until you can't twist anymore. Tie or tape the stick down so it doesn't fly loose. No better clamp was ever devised! And look no farther than your clothes basket when you need a very *small* clamp. I've found that ordinary spring clothespins are great for little jobs.

Protecting Fireplace From Stain

Proud as punch of that new fireplace? Protect it from the inevitable soot and smoke by brushing a solution made from half penetrating wood sealer and half turpentine onto the clean dry bricks.

You can freshen up a fireplace that's already sooty by scrubbing the bricks with a solution of one cup of washing *soda* to a pail of water.

Securing Lopsided Pictures

If you have a picture that takes a decided tilt due north every time the commuter's local roars by, run, don't walk, to the dime store for a lump of florist's clay. Stick a blob on the back of the frame and press firmly against the wall. No more whopper-jawed pictures!

Attaching Cup Hooks to Plaster

Plaster walls are great, and durable, and lovely, and all that. But they've caused more than one woman to lose her temper when she tried to install a simple little cup hook to hold back the kitchen curtains. Try this the next time, and save all that agitation. Just stick a lump of plastic wood onto the plaster where you want to place the cup hook. Wait a day for it to dry, then screw the cup hook into the plastic wood!

Ridding Closets of Mildew

Mildew is caused by dampness. You can help keep your closets mildew-free in damp weather by leaving a light bulb burning continously in the closet, with the door closed. Be sure the bulb doesn't touch any of your flowery finery up there on that top shelf. Fire, you know!

Concealing Edges of Plywood Shelves

Making plywood shelves is easy. It's trying to finish off the miserable edges that will drive you to look up a solution in this book! Of course, if the shelves are hanging in your French Provincial living room I'd suggest you do the job right and edge each one with an attractive wooden molding or some of that flexible wood-grain edging from the lumber company. But if you're in a hurry and a slap-dash job is in order, just press on edging of colorful vinyl tape. It'll stick tight and look pretty until you have time to give a permanent edging.

Fixing Squeaky Stairs

Stairs usually squeak when their wedges (some construction parts underneath the staircase) come loose. Sometimes it's possible to reset those wedges, sometimes it's not. It all depends on whether or not you can get under the staircase. But you can probably stop those annoying squeaks yourself by just hammering some eightpenny finishing nails through the front of the tread into the riser. (The tread is the part you step on, the riser is the vertical board between treads.) Put at least four or five nails through each tread.

Relieving Pounding Noise in Radiator

That hammering noise in your radiator, which is just slightly below the legal limit for planes breaking the sound barrier, isn't nearly as serious as it sounds. Check to see if the shut-off valve is opened or closed *all the way*. It must be one or the other, depending upon whether you're using the heat or not. If that doesn't cure the iron monster, the chances are the pounding is caused by water trapped in the radiator and its connecting pipe. All you need to do is tilt the radiator a bit so that water drains back to the boiler. You're going to scrounge up a few thin pieces of wood and push them under the legs at the opposite end of the radiator from where the steam pipe is connected. Start with one, and if that doesn't stop the noise, add another, and another, until peace and harmony reign again. You might try paint paddles, a yardstick cut in half, the end of one of those wooden boxes used to ship fruit (from the produce department of the corner grocery), or a stack of those acid rock records your demented roommate or incorrigible teenager dragged home.

Silencing a Noisy Window Air Conditioner

If the noise is *inside* the air conditioner unit, it probably needs lubrication and you'll have to call a serviceman. If it seems to be in the framework of the machine, the chances are it is vibrating like crazy and needs a tranquilizing treatment. Check to see if it is securely fastened to the window. Tighten any loose screws or expanding plates. Then, get some rope caulking (see the chapter on the outdoors) from the hardware store and pack it tightly around the unit until there is no movement while the machine is in operation. You should notice a big difference. And, you'll wonder why you put up with that racket so long!

Tricky Tool Tips

A broom handle makes an excellent straight-edge when you need a long length for marking.

Save that old vegetable grater. It makes a handy file to smooth rough edges off things (Fig. 15-4).

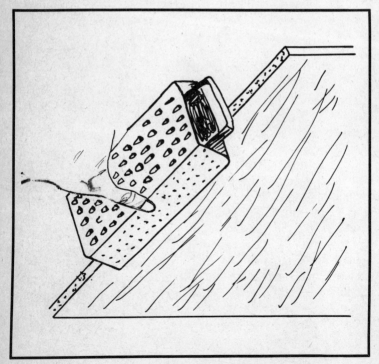

Fig. 15-4. A vegetable grater can be used to smooth edges.

Put a rubber crutch tip over the end of your hammer handle. You'll have a handy padded "persuader" to use when forcing things you don't want to mar.

Find another rough spot on that desk you're refinishing? And you've used the last of the sandpaper? Fish around in your purse for an emery board. It works fine.

Use a wide-bladed chisel or putty knife when prying off delicate objects which are to be re-used (thin moldings, dainty carvings, etc.). This saves damaging them, which is almost a certainty if you use a screwdriver.

Index